Flexible Mindsets in Schools

Flexible Mindsets in Schools abandons painstaking evolution in favour of a bold, transformative revolution. It blends research and easily implementable practice to drive solutions that give learners and educators the freedom to become self-directed: to unleash questioning, problem-solving and creativity.

This key text explores how to blend existing and new practices and unlock the potential of student agency as the pathway towards resilience and adaptation. The Flexible Mindsets Model fuses three components that rely on each other to drive self-directed learning: metacognition, "I CAN" mindset messages and executive function processes. This book presents a roadmap for how to create an environment and culture where learners are aware of what works when, feel safe to take learning-related risks, believe that they are capable and have the tools they need to learn.

Flexible Mindsets in Schools will give educators hope that there is a way to revolutionise education to meet the needs of students during these uncertain times by taking small, manageable steps.

Julie Dunstan is a developmental psychologist and the Founding Director of reFLEXions®, an initiative designed to develop Flexible Mindsets for self-directed learning.

Susannah Cole is an executive function coach and Managing Director of reFLEXions®.

Flexible Mindsets in Schools

Channelling Brain Power for Critical Thinking, Complex Problem-Solving and Creativity

Julie Dunstan and Susannah Cole

LONDON AND NEW YORK

First published 2022
by Routledge
2 Park Square, Milton Park, Abingdon, Oxon OX14 4RN

and by Routledge
605 Third Avenue, New York, NY 10158

Routledge is an imprint of the Taylor & Francis Group, an informa business

© 2022 Julie Dunstan and Susannah Cole

The right of Julie Dunstan and Susannah Cole to be identified as authors of this work has been asserted by them in accordance with sections 77 and 78 of the Copyright, Designs and Patents Act 1988.

All rights reserved. No part of this book may be reprinted or reproduced or utilised in any form or by any electronic, mechanical, or other means, now known or hereafter invented, including photocopying and recording, or in any information storage or retrieval system, without permission in writing from the publishers.

Trademark notice: Product or corporate names may be trademarks or registered trademarks, and are used only for identification and explanation without intent to infringe.

British Library Cataloguing-in-Publication Data
A catalogue record for this book is available from the British Library

Library of Congress Cataloging-in-Publication Data
Names: Dunstan, Julie (Psychologist), author. | Cole, Susannah, author.
Title: Flexible mindsets in schools : channelling brain power for critical thinking, complex problem-solving and creativity / Julie Dunstan and Susannah Cole.
Description: Abingdon, Oxon ; New York, NY : Routledge, 2022. | Includes bibliographical references and index. |
Identifiers: LCCN 2021024285 | ISBN 9781032069760 (hardback) | ISBN 9781032069777 (paperback) | ISBN 9781003204817 (ebook)
Subjects: LCSH: Critical thinking—Study and teaching. | Problem solving—Study and teaching. | Creative ability—Study and teaching. | Metacognition. | Self-culture.
Classification: LCC LB1590.3 .D86 2022 | DDC 370.15/2—dc23
LC record available at https://lccn.loc.gov/2021024285

ISBN: 978-1-032-06976-0 (hbk)
ISBN: 978-1-032-06977-7 (pbk)
ISBN: 978-1-003-20481-7 (ebk)

DOI: 10.4324/9781003204817

Typeset in Bembo and Helvetica Neue
by Apex CoVantage, LLC

Contents

About the authors — viii
List of figures — x
List of tables — xi
Opening: why channel brain power for the 3<u>C</u>'s? — xii
Acknowledgements — xvi

Section I. Flexible Mindsets: Where do we begin? — 1

1 What is a Flexible Mindset? The journey of self-directed learning — 3

Self-directed learning — 4
Flexible Mindsets and metacognition — 6
Flexible Mindsets and I CAN messages — 9
Flexible Mindsets and executive function processes — 12
The Flexible Mindsets Spiral of Reflective Learning: get started with Flexible Mindsets — 19

2 What is the mechanism for Flexible Mindsets? Productive Puzzling and curiosity — 24

Why is curiosity so important for deeper thinking and learning? — 25
What happens in the brain when we puzzle? — 26
Guidelines for piquing curiosity — 28
What are the necessary conditions for Productive Puzzling? — 31

Section II. Productive Puzzling conditions for transforming mindsets — 39

3 How do fixed mentalities close the window for learning? — 41

Fear of failure — 42

	How do power and control close the window for learning?	46
	Values that close the window for learning	48
4	Building trusting relationships to open the window for learning (condition 1)	54
	Hitting the kill switch	54
	Trusting relationships	55
	How do co-creation and power sharing open the window for learning?	57
	Values that open the window for learning	59
	Flexible Mindsets language	62
5	The superstructure of Productive Puzzling (conditions 2, 3, 4 and 5)	68
	Valuing practice and struggle	69
	How to teach students about strategies	70
	Carefully Crafted Questions for exploring the 3C's	72
	Flexible Mindsets feedback: perseverance PLUS flexible strategy use	75

Section III. Productive Puzzling in action: How do we target the 3C's?   83

	Criteria for Flexible Mindsets strategies	83
	The 3C's in action	84
6	Critical Thinking: Does it make sense?	85
	Flexible Mindsets definition of Critical Thinking	87
	How do questions help the brain learn?	88
	Metacognition applied to Critical Thinking	88
	Flexible Mindset strategies for Critical Thinking	89
	Critical Thinking in action: a social justice example from grade 1	95
	Productive Puzzling and Critical Thinking: retrieval practice	96
7	Complex Problem-Solving: What else can we try?	99
	Flexible Mindsets definition of Complex Problem-Solving	101
	What happens in the brain when we solve complex problems?	103
	Metacognition applied to Complex Problem-Solving	103
	Flexible Mindset strategies for Complex Problem-Solving	106
	Complex Problem-Solving in the moment: an energy solution from an eight-year-old	110
	Productive Puzzling for Complex Problem-Solving: retrieval practice	111
8	Creativity: What are the possibilities?	114
	Flexible Mindsets definition of Creativity	116
	What happens in the brain when we imagine?	117

Metacognition applied to <u>C</u>reativity	117
Flexible Mindsets strategies for <u>C</u>reativity	119
<u>C</u>reativity in action: a space junk example from a teenager	123
Productive Puzzling for <u>C</u>reativity: retrieval practice	124

Section IV. Flexible Mindsets for equitable education: How can we use the 3<u>C</u>'s for the benefit of all learners?   129

  9   Equitable classrooms for teaching the 3<u>C</u>'s in the context of uncertainty   131

What about the 'high flyers'? The fixed mentalities of high achievers	133
'What if?' versus 'what if?' Relieving anxiety during times of uncertainty	135
Students with 'Fix-lexia': learning differences and <u>C</u>reativity	136
Persevērance versus Persĕverance: flexibility as an antidote to rigid thinking (pr·suh·veer·uhns versus pr·sev·eh·rents)	138
The digital double down and the therapeutic potential of empathy	141

  10   System disruption for equitable education   147

Educational purpose and design	148
Suspect policies and practices	149
How do we disrupt?	155
Imagine the possibilities (be <u>C</u>reative)	159

Glossary	*162*
Appendix A: The Flexible Mindsets Spiral of Reflective Learning	*165*
Appendix B: Metacognitive Insights Survey (MIS)	*166*
Appendix C: Flexible Learning Activation Checklist (FLAC)	*168*
Index	*170*

About the authors

Julie Dunstan

Psychologist and author, Dr Julie Dunstan believes that the essence of equity lies in equipping all learners with the tools they need to respond adaptively and resiliently to the adversity of today's complex and ever-changing world. For decades, she has partnered in a wide range of community settings to engage children, families and organisations in self-discovery and finding a pathway towards autonomy. All of her work is grounded in forging trusting relationships that create space for everyone to ask questions, make mistakes and take risks for learning.

Julie holds an MA in early childhood and a PhD in educational psychology. She has conducted policy research on child development, family needs, addictions, literacy amongst inmates, learning differences and general education. Julie has lectured at the undergraduate and graduate levels in psychology, education and organisational development. She has also presented internationally at professional conferences and research-based symposiums and contributed to published resources for educators.

Julie has translated research into practice by driving innovations such as the ICAN Math programme and the I PLAY early childhood pre-reading intervention. In 2015, she also founded the reFLEXions® initiative, a team that builds Flexible Mindsets to reframe teaching as the pathway towards resilience and adaptability. Her purpose is to elevate those around her and propel them to direct their own learning journeys.

Susannah Cole

Susannah Cole is an author and executive function coach who partners with students to explore systems, habits and mindsets that facilitate learning HOW to learn.

Through building trusting relationships, she empowers students to set meaningful goals and actively direct their learning towards fulfilling their personal aspirations.

As the managing director of reFLEXions®, she works alongside a team to provide resources, professional coaching and consultation to build Flexible Mindsets that help educators to reframe teaching as an equitable pathway towards building resilience and adaptability for ALL students. Susannah holds a MEd in developmental psychology and has grown her expertise throughout the past 25 years working in the field of education. She has taught at all levels from preschool through college. For decades, she worked in educational settings as an early childhood educator, integrated middle school teacher at the IB level, a specialised autism therapist, learning support teacher and college professor.

With the aim of making learning engaging and accessible to all students, Susannah has served as an educational consultant to families, educators and schools. Through workshops, peer mentoring and international presentations, she has spearheaded efforts to build professional learning and coaching communities. Her calling is to transform classrooms into spaces that centre responsiveness, relevance and curiosity and where we can bring all of ourselves to our learning.

Figures

1.1	Metacognition: the first step in self-directed learning	8
1.2	I CAN mindset messages	9
1.3	Key executive function processes	13
1.4	Working memory in action	15
1.5	The Flexible Mindsets model	19
1.6	The Flexible Mindsets Spiral of Reflective Learning	20
2.1	The evolutionary value of NOT thinking	27
2.2	The five conditions for Productive Puzzling	32
2.3	Productive Puzzling balances challenge with solutions that are within reach	33
3.1	Closing the window for learning	45
3.2	The 'sweet spot' for learning	46
4.1	Trusting relationships: condition 1 for Productive Puzzling	55
4.2	Uncertainties about power sharing in the classroom	58
4.3	Flexible Mindsets language that builds trust	62
5.1	The superstructure for Productive Puzzling: conditions 2, 3, 4 and 5	68
5.2	The Flexible Mindsets bidirectional questioning taxonomy	74
5.3	Perseverance PLUS flexible strategy use equals resilience and adaptability	78
6.1	Critical Thinking: *Does it make sense?*	86
7.1	Complex Problem-Solving: *What else can we try?*	100
8.1	Creativity: *What are the possibilities?*	115
9.1	Equality versus equity	131
9.2	Implications of mindsets for diverse learners	134
9.3	Persĕverance: being stuck in the mud	139
10.1	Steps for system disruption	156

Tables

1.1	The Flexible Mindsets Spiral of Reflective Learning: get started with Flexible Mindsets	21
2.1	The Flexible Mindsets Spiral of Reflective Learning: Productive Puzzling	35
3.1	The Flexible Mindsets Spiral of Reflective Learning: closing the window for learning	51
4.1	The Flexible Mindsets Spiral of Reflective Learning: opening the window for learning	65
5.1	Examples of strategies for everyday goals	72
5.2	The Flexible Mindsets Spiral of Reflective Learning: the superstructure of Productive Puzzling	79
	Section III Introduction Table 1: Flexible Mindsets summary of the 3C's	84
6.1	Metacognitive Insights Survey (MIS): Critical Thinking	89
6.2	*Prove it!* What invention has most changed the way we live?	93
6.3	Flexible Learning Activation Checklist (FLAC): Critical Thinking	96
6.4	Productive Puzzling and Critical Thinking: retrieval practice	97
7.1	Flexible Mindsets criteria for complex problems	102
7.2	Metacognitive Insights Survey (MIS): Complex Problem-Solving	104
7.3	'Fork in the Road' strategy for Complex Problem-Solving	108
7.4	Flexible Learning Activation Checklist (FLAC): Complex Problem-Solving	111
7.5	Productive Puzzling and Complex Problem-Solving: retrieval practice	111
8.1	Metacognitive Insights Survey (MIS): Creativity	118
8.2	Flexible Learning Activation Checklist (FLAC): Creativity	124
8.3	Productive Puzzling and Creativity: retrieval practice	125

Opening: why channel brain power for the 3<u>C</u>'s?

The premise of this book starts with an invitation to all educators to ask ourselves, "What is it that we do to children when we *educate* them?"

> When children are very young, they have natural curiosities about the world and explore them, trying diligently to figure out what is real. As they become 'producers' they fall away from exploration and start fishing for the right answers with little thought. They believe they must always be right. . . . They believe the only good response from the teacher is 'yes' and that a 'no' is a defeat.
>
> (John Holt)

What we do when we *educate* children is to convert them away from being learners to become producers. We chop them up into pieces, some of which aren't welcome at school, and then we chop up the curriculum into arbitrary pieces that make no sense to children and are not relevant to their lived experiences. We mass produce students and then ask them to take initiative and think outside the box. Holt's concerns resonate with the authors of this book whose histories, although very different, have led them to question the practices and policies that constrain our children. Here are our stories.

Julie's story

As a young psychologist, I struggled with the disconnect between my beliefs about children and learning and the requirements of the system. Having been trained in university, medical and community settings, I should have felt well prepared for my career. But I just couldn't shake the feeling that something was terribly wrong. In a helping organisation that served children and families, I was expected to do assessments that helped children learn better. But why did we end up reducing children to numbers?

Why were decisions based on how fast children worked, their stores of factual knowledge and their compliance, at the expense of social problem-solving, deeper exploration and creativity? I ended up following a path that showed me the entirety of the system in one community: from early intervention through all stages of the public school system to lecturing in education, psychology and programme evaluation. I worked with nonprofits and conducted research with families, inmates and those who struggle with addictions. With all of this experience and application, I kept coming back to the same thoughts. If we love our children and care about their learning, why do we lock them into prisons of self-doubt? We know what it takes to thrive in this world: *resilience* and *flexibility*. What will it take for us to give *all* children the tools they need to feel safe to explore and to be adaptable in the face of adversity?

Susannah's story

In contrast, I started out in early childhood where I taught children in ways that reflected my core beliefs about how children learn best and I had the freedom to be creative and playful with the delivery of curriculum. My early career in Canada, training early childhood educators in the college setting, proved to me how publicly funded, all-day early learning could help all students begin their schooling with a strong foundation that fosters learning, development, health and holistic wellbeing. These experiences inspired me to believe in the possibility of a society where structural inequities would not impede learning.

During my early career, I also independently pursued my passion for restorative justice practices which led to an ongoing journey of exploring the different ways I could be an agent of change within punitive, inhumane systems. However, working outside the sheltered walls of academia challenged me to confront the realities of a system built on a Western worldview which sustained privilege based in gender, race and economics. This became even more evident when I taught in elementary and middle school. I felt trapped in a system that didn't provide the time or resources to meet students where they were. I found myself having to teach required objectives that weren't relevant to the children, setting up incentive programmes and giving grades that didn't reflect what students were capable of. Ultimately, I ended up disheartened by the lack of tools and support to implement what I knew the students needed most: to be heard and seen by a responsive teacher who delivers meaningful content and inspires them to want to be self-directed learners who make a difference in the world.

As two white, unconventional, female educators with advanced degrees and decades of experience working with marginalised children, we had crossed paths with each other along the way. We recognised each other as kindred spirits who believed in connecting with the humanness in everyone. We discovered that we shared a vision for education that made learning accessible to all children. We agreed that there is nothing wrong with those learners who struggle in schools. *It is the system that needs to change.* The goals for education need to be transformed to ensure that students love learning and are active, resilient and adaptable. So we set about creating a framework for reshaping belief systems and developing alternative assessment methods, research, coaching and educational practices. We envisioned a way to bring all of ourselves to experience curiosity and trial and error as more valuable than being a speedy 'producer' of the one right answer. We called this Flexible Mindsets.

We have continued our Flexible Mindsets journey by providing coaching for students and teachers, conducting research, producing resources and presenting our work internationally. This book is the culmination of our decades of experience in education and captures our combined expertise and shared beliefs.

At the core of our story are today's children who, as adults, will be required to solve complex problems unimagined by previous generations. These will include pandemics, racial injustices, climate change and rapidly increasing economic gaps. They are also likely to have opportunities to shape the world in ways that we cannot imagine. They are the future innovators of nanotechnology, artificial intelligence, sustainable environmental policies, cyber law enforcement, criminal reform and fields that have not yet been conceived.

The reality is that educational systems have not kept pace with the changing needs of children in our complex and ever-shifting world. A century ago, education for all meant ensuring that students mastered the basics of the 3R's: Reading, wRiting and 'Rithmetic. Society and the economy required sameness and conformity. Independent exploration was frowned upon or reserved for scholars. In today's context, overemphasis on the 3R's no longer serves anyone well. What all learners really need are the capacities required for responding adaptively to uncertainty and adversity: Critical Thinking, Complex Problem-Solving and Creativity: what we call the 3C's.

Today's teachers work within a rigid structure that follows an overloaded curriculum with unrealistic benchmarks. The pressure to produce standardised results forces a one-size-fits-all approach that stifles creativity, other ways of knowing and out-of-the-box thinking. This leaves no room for educators to trust what they know, reach children and learn alongside them. The typical education system is built on the behaviourist principles of token systems, rewards and punishment. It promotes standardised, number-based decision making as a proxy for equality. Rather than follow the status quo, educators are beginning to challenge themselves to be authentic, stretch their minds and trust their intuition. If education is to be equitable, student engagement must be driven by curiosity and meaningful questions that shift ownership of learning from the teacher to a student-teacher partnership. The remedy lies in using Flexible Mindsets to teach students to learn HOW to learn and ultimately become self-determining.

For every teacher who is committed to equitable education and believes that all children are capable, this book provides the essential tools for learners to become resilient, shift perspectives and direct their own learning journey.

You may notice in this book that some of our ideas are consistent with other educational approaches. The novelty of this book lies in how we bend and blend existing approaches and hone in on the agency of becoming self-directed. We wrote this book with three purposes in mind:

- to reframe teaching as the pathway towards resilience and flexibility for surmounting uncertain futures;
- to shift the focus of learning from the 3R's to the 3C's (Critical Thinking, Complex Problem-Solving and Creativity); and
- to debunk myths about learning and interrupt systems that are inequitable and stifle original ideas.

Our call is to abandon painstaking evolution in favour of a bold, transformative revolution. The time for tinkering is over! Rather than becoming discouraged by the obstacles to systemic change, we offer you tools to empower your students in your classroom, here and now. We blend research with humanness to drive solutions that give learners and educators the freedom to become self-directed: to unleash *questioning, problem-solving* and *imagination*.

Acknowledgements

We owe our biggest debt to all the students and their families who have shaped our mindsets over the past three decades. You are the inspiration for this book. Your talents, persistence and out-of-the-box thinking have driven us to recognise that all children should be seen and heard and that we should be able to bring all of ourselves to our learning experiences.

We would also like to thank all our friends and colleagues, most especially Dr Lynn Meltzer and her team at the Institutes for Learning and Development, Gretchen Wegner and the members of her professional learning community and The Reading Clinic. Our work has benefited immensely from our dialogue with you, your willingness to act as a sounding board and your generosity in sharing your own professional experiences.

To Anna, our graphic designer, we thank you for your Creativity and flexibility. Your ability to capture the essence of our vision in images has greatly amplified our ability to communicate our message in meaningful and powerful ways.

We would also like to express our gratitude to all the educators and principals who have welcomed us into your schools. You have grappled with the actualisation of Flexible Mindsets, implemented and adapted our strategies and provided the essential input needed to translate our model to the real world and classroom context.

Many of our friends and colleagues have kindly reviewed all or part of this book, simply out of your goodwill. Your contributions and feedback at various stages of our journey have enabled us to sharpen and enrich our endeavours. Thank you.

Finally, we could not have written this book without the support and love of our families and friends. Thank you for knowing our true selves and indulging us in our ways of being.

Acknowledgements

We'd like to thank Sarah Hyde, at Routledge, for her recognition of the value of this book. We would also like to thank our Senior Editor, Bruce Roberts, and our Editorial Assistant, Molly Selby. The entire team were incredibly responsive and insightful as they moved us from a rough draft through to a published resource. Without you, *Flexible Mindsets in Schools* may never have reached a worldwide audience and realised its potential to reframe education as the pathway towards resilience and flexibility.

SECTION

Flexible Mindsets
Where do we begin?

CHAPTER

What is a Flexible Mindset? The journey of self-directed learning

On a recent visit to a preschool, I was chatting with one of my colleagues. I noticed that she was stretching her arms frequently and rubbing her biceps. I asked her if she had recently had a strenuous workout at the gym. She shared the following story:

> I was on the playground with several children. We had been exploring the properties of various materials and some foam cubes had ended up in a tree. We identified this as a puzzle to solve. I tried stretching up, but could not reach the branches. "How could we solve this puzzle?" I asked. One child suggested getting something for me to stand on. I concluded that this was good problem-solving and started to head over to get a stepping stool. "Ms Raynor," another child said, "Be flexible! You could just lift me up and I can get them!"

This anecdote illustrates this preschooler's ability to shift perspectives and adapt while learning. She asks herself, *What else can we try?* when faced with a puzzle (how do we get the foam squares?). She is able to help generate more than one strategy for solving the puzzle (getting a stepping stool, holding a child up to reach the squares). She is already developing the 3C's: Critical Thinking, Complex Problem-Solving and Creativity. She is predisposed to direct her own learning and to develop a sense of competence.

> Seth's mother realised early on that, despite his high intelligence, her son struggled to understand the instructions for school projects. His products did not reflect his abilities and he left key components out of his assignments. Seeing his frustration, she did what most mothers would do: she helped. It started out with suggesting one or two additions to his work. As the demands of school increased, his mother ended up helping more and more with Seth's work. Seth discovered shortcuts when doing research for his projects like watching YouTube videos instead of reading research articles. He would appear lost in

DOI: 10.4324/9781003204817-2

class and would ask for help before giving it a real try on his own. This encouraged his teachers to also jump in and help him. Without the opportunities to work through complex, multi-step tasks, Seth's brain did not develop the capacity to think critically, try different strategies and persevere. By the time he was in high school, Seth had no idea how to get started with an assignment and he did not view himself as capable. He became overwhelmed by worrisome thoughts and was eventually diagnosed with an anxiety disorder.

In today's world, we have immediate access to unlimited amounts of information. We have created a climate of convenience where children expect instant answers and have a low tolerance for frustration. They are allowed to be passive in their learning and are not being empowered to think for themselves. Neurologically, they are being disadvantaged by not developing the capacities that help them to plan, organise, problem solve and make decisions (Sweetland & Stolberg 2015). Ironically, curricular demands are substantially more complex and getting into college is more difficult than ever. These opposing forces clash and our children are the collateral damage.

This dynamic perpetuates and, in some cases, exacerbates, social injustices. It discourages ways of being that create the conditions in which students have a sense of autonomy and show us how competent they are. We are denying our children the pathway towards self-determination.

> In this chapter, we:
>
> 1   provide the Flexible Mindsets definition of self-directed learning;
> 2   highlight metacognition as the foundation for Flexible Mindsets;
> 3   briefly review the importance of I CAN messages in developing Flexible Mindsets;
> 4   show how executive function processes offer essential tools for Flexible Mindsets; and
> 5   introduce the Flexible Mindsets Spiral of Reflective Learning.

How can we, as mere individuals, without simply rebranding existing ideologies, transform those belief systems that are entrenched in the matrix?

Self-directed learning

We can transform mindsets at both the individual and systemic level by creating a culture around learning HOW to learn.

Over the past several years, our team has been studying this phenomenon and translating our discoveries into principles and practices that transform learning environments. We use the term Flexible Mindsets to refer to the metacognitive awareness, I CAN messages and executive function processes that are necessary for self-directed learning. *When self-directed, learners actively focus mental energy on their goals and apply their learning to new and meaningful contexts, even when challenged; they are driven by curiosity, a desire to grow and the love of learning!*

This definition of self-directed learning pulls from Self-Determination Theory and its framework for understanding the factors that promote motivation (Ryan & Deci 2017). Self-Determination Theory refers to three basic psychological needs: autonomy, competence and relatedness. This is why, in our model, we emphasise building skills within the context of trusting relationships (National Scientific Council on the Developing Child 2015). Understanding how these needs impact motivation is vital if we want learners to become self-directed.

Inherent in the definition of self-directed learning is the shift from passive to active learning and this is at the core of a Flexible Mindset. Active learners dig in, grapple with information, seek to uncover what they don't know and make mistakes. This requires mental effort and perseverance.

By uncovering what they don't know, learners can free themselves from preconceived notions of intelligence and exercise flexibility in selecting, applying and modifying strategies for learning. If we present not knowing as nonthreatening, this creates openings for wonder and curiosity. "If knowledge is power, knowing what we don't know is wisdom" (Grant 2021). The very act of learning HOW to learn changes your brain and makes you smarter.

Questions are at the heart of this shift from passive to active learning. There is a powerful moment that occurs in our brain when it switches from receiving information to inquiring. Questions are the guiding force leading to self-directed learning and self-determination. *Does it make sense? What else could we try? What are the possibilities?* These three questions are the hallmarks of Flexible Mindsets. Asking questions puts the learner in charge by requiring them to explore their existing knowledge, make connections, solve problems and share ideas. Strategies are the tools we use to support students to become self-directed learners who think critically, solve complex problems and are creative.

Beyond questions, using strategies is an integral part of active learning. When flexible minds get together, strategies are expected to be shown, viewed, commented on, highlighted and celebrated! No more hiding our fingers under the table when we use them to count. Overt strategy use is the signature characteristic of accomplished learners. Strategies are different from skills. A skill is a sequence of steps that has become routine and does not require conscious thought to implement. Strategies are what we use when a solution is not automatically obvious. *Strategies are deliberate, goal-directed attempts that require mental effort: they are what we use when we don't know.*

So, how do we get learners to think about, apply and adapt strategies to reach goals?

We need a framework that informs the practices we use every day. A framework that reflects our commitment to an environment where students can bring all of themselves and take ownership of their learning. In the Flexible Mindsets model, we use three components that rely on each other to drive self-directed learning and empower students:

1   metacognition;
2   I CAN messages; and
3   executive function processes.

These three areas have often been treated as distinct constructs in research and practice, each with their own value for learning. In the Flexible Mindsets model, all three are inextricably linked and influence and reinforce each other. This chapter explains the theoretical framework underpinning the Flexible Mindset practices that guide our team's professional exchanges and the development of our educational resources.

Flexible Mindsets and metacognition

Educational empowerment starts with the awareness and knowledge needed to identify and resolve challenges that occur naturally as we learn new material or solve novel problems. It is imperative that a learner begin with a desire to explore questions such as *Who am I as a learner? What are my strengths? How do I understand the thoughts of others? What strategy could I try?* Before individuals can take charge of their own learning, they must develop awareness of themselves and possess knowledge of a variety of factors that influence learning (Meltzer 2010). Knowing how our brains learn is just the beginning because that information is useless unless we know how to apply it.

> Brian had a backpack full of loose papers. If he did put his papers away, he put them in an overstuffed plastic pouch with a zipper. He was introduced to a binder system with colour coded dividers for each subject. After using the system for a week, it was clear that this would not work for Brian. He had simply put all the loose papers inside the binder (without actually clipping them in the rings). He explained how most of his teachers didn't hand out papers that were already punched and that it was difficult for him to open and close the binder and even to line up all the holes properly. He just wasn't going to use this system.

For Brian, one of the most common strategies recommended for organisation didn't work. When presented with a variety of other possible strategies, he asked if he could try an accordion file instead. He labelled each file with a subject and had no problem putting the papers in the correct subject during each class. He used this system successfully for the rest of the school year.

Megacognition is the part of our world knowledge that has to do with people as active learners and their awareness of tasks, goals, actions and experiences (Flavell 1981). It is the understanding of what you know and where you're going, as well as the knowledge of what's needed to get there (Taylor 1999). It is through this knowledge that a learner is expected to activate and adapt strategies to overcome a difficult situation.

> When doing her math homework, Ayana moves fluently through a series of simple word problems that require the addition of two single digit numbers. She is adept at solving these questions by adding the numbers in her head and simply writing down the answer. As she progresses, the items become more complex: there are many more details in the stories that are distracting; there are more than two numbers; and the numbers are multidigit. Ayana begins to struggle to prioritise the relevant details, keep track of the numbers in her head and which step she is on in the algorithm. (Uh, oh! These are trickier questions and I can't do them in my head.) This Metacognitive Insight leads her to see that her strategy is no longer effective and guides her to use her knowledge of strategies to explore other ways to solve the problem. Without these metacognitive experiences and knowledge, Ayana would be unable to switch to a more effective strategy.

'Metacognitive experiences' are conscious feelings that happen as we learn (Flavell 1981). For example, feeling that you do or do not understand or feeling hesitant about the choice you have made. By recognising and accurately interpreting these experiences, a learner can activate knowledge for learning new material, solving problems and being creative. We use the term *Metacognitive Insights* to refer exclusively to those *'Uh-oh' moments when we notice that what we're doing isn't working and engage in honest self-reflection about our own learning.*

In traditional models, metacognitive knowledge deals mainly with mental processes such as knowledge about one's own learning-related processes and the strategies that assist performance (Flavell 2000). Our Flexible Mindsets approach to metacognition is also influenced by the research on theory of mind. The term theory of mind refers to our understanding that people have different wants, beliefs, thoughts, motivations, knowledge and moods. This ability facilitates our social behaviour and social understanding through the interpretation and prediction of what other people are thinking and feeling (Premack & Woodruff 1978; Baron-Cohen 1995; Gweon & Saxe 2013). Since learning and problem-solving often occur at the interpersonal level, insights regarding one's own thoughts and experiences is only half of the equation. If learning is to occur through interactions with others, then an awareness of the thoughts of others is also critical (Winner 2007). Learners who have difficulty with perspective taking struggle to understand the big picture and to produce output for assignments. Perspective taking incorporates reflection about differing viewpoints across cultural divides and over time. This is a prerequisite condition for equitable learning.

> Amelia was writing a graphic novel exploring emigration and its impact on families. She was excited to think about the journey and all the possibilities moving to a new country provided, but when she started to write the actual conversation between family members, she had difficulty including dialogue that captured their different points of view (those who stayed in their home country versus those who moved) as well as their corresponding experiences and emotions with consideration given to the historical context.

In essence, self-awareness is built upon an understanding of who we are as learners, especially personal strengths and challenges; our abilities to have insights about the thoughts of others; and our knowledge of which strategies work best in a given context (see Figure 1.1). Developing metacognitive understanding empowers us to become advocates for our own learning, charting the path towards becoming self-directed. Learners can only move along the course towards self-advocacy if, together, we identify strengths, share with others and take action accordingly.

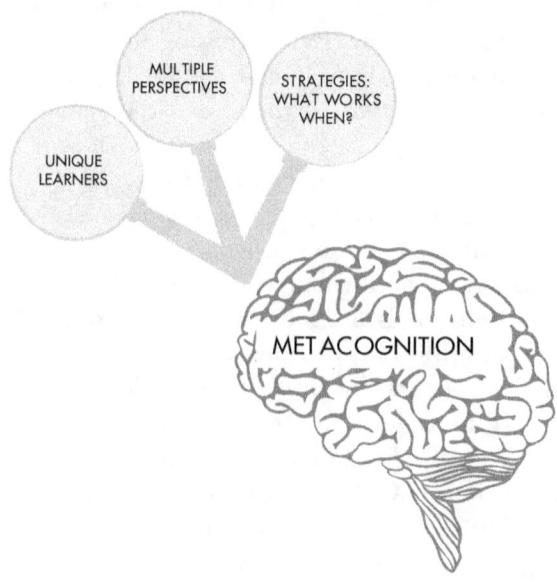

Figure 1.1 Metacognition: the first step in self-directed learning

Metacognition is the awareness of one's own learning and thinking. It is our ability to ponder when we face puzzles. It serves as the underlying cornerstone for mindsets and executive function processes. From our decades of working with diverse learners, one thing has become clear: you can know your learning profile and you can even know which strategies will help you; but, in order to use those strategies, you must first believe in yourself and know that you can get smarter. In the next section, we will explore the impact of I CAN messages on closing or opening the window on learning.

Flexible Mindsets and I CAN messages

Bernard Beckett (2006, p. 7) writes,

> Human spirit is the ability to face the uncertainty of the future with curiosity and optimism. It is the belief that problems can be solved, differences resolved. It is a type of confidence. And it is fragile. It can be blackened by fear and superstition.

In this way, he illustrates the power of mindset messages as formulated in our model (see Figure 1.2).

Self-directed learners know how to construct their own solutions and build bridges that lead to successes they can claim as their own. They have learned to be resourceful by working through life's ongoing series of miscalculations, mistakes and setbacks. If we deny children these experiences, we deprive them of believing

Figure 1.2 I CAN mindset messages

in themselves. As adults, the drive to help can be potent, but our restraint is the gift that propels children towards perseverance, innovation and resilience (Goldstein & Brooks 2013).

> Jelani was a new student in middle school. He began the year eager to learn and excited by the idea of a rotating schedule with a variety of teachers. The window was wide open for learning. By the beginning of October, the complexity of the curriculum and increasing workload started to overwhelm Jelani.

As learners become more metacognitively aware, we often expect an immediate improvement in their abilities to deal with a large volume of reading, comprehend complex vocabulary, understand complicated assignments, complete long-term projects, perform on tests and learn independently. Metacognition alone rarely produces these results. In order to respond positively to challenging problems, learners must be resilient (Brooks & Goldstein 2002). *A resilient mindset is the product of equipping learners with the necessary tools to work adaptively through change, adversity, trauma, threats, challenges and chronic stress that lie in their pathway towards purposeful self-direction.* Resilient learners are hopeful and possess high self-worth. They are more likely to view mistakes, hardships and obstacles as challenges to confront rather than as stressors to avoid (Brooks 2015). It's important to note that there are also instances in which a person cannot simply avoid stressors like sexism, racism and other aggressions.

> For example, many of Jelani's stressors happened at school. He struggled to focus during lessons, often daydreaming and missing large chunks of information. When he wasn't daydreaming, he found himself thinking about all the things he needed to do and worrying about what was coming next. There were a couple of teachers he thought didn't like him because they had noticed him daydreaming during their lessons and he could tell they were getting frustrated with his lack of focus. His window for learning had started to close.
>
> It wasn't long before Jelani woke up dreading school and mornings around his house became a battle of wills. His responses to his parents and sister were short and he often snapped at them in an angry tone. Lively discussions and jokes during family time were becoming rare. Most of the conversation at home focused on what he wasn't doing and how he needed to spend more time doing schoolwork and less time playing video games. Jelani was desperate to escape the pressure he was feeling. Video games were the only time his mind would stop spinning with everything he had to do and he could feel a sense of control. His window for learning was now half closed.

We now know that fixed mentalities do not serve anyone well. It is growth mindsets that allow us to plunge into something wholeheartedly and stick to it even when it is not something we are good at (Dweck 2008). Growth mindsets do not impose limitations upon an individual's capabilities. People with growth mindsets believe that their own successes depend primarily on factors such as practice, perseverance and resilience. As adults, we need to ensure that we avoid both the rescue trap (where we send the message that a child is not capable), as well as the blaming trap (where we urge children to 'get grit' without teaching them HOW to learn). In a world where adaptability is critical for individual and collective success, it becomes essential to tailor educational experiences to foster growth, rather than fixed, mindsets. If we wait too long to cultivate a culture of Flexible Mindsets, as was the case for Jelani, the window for learning will close.

If we are to commit to transforming mindsets, we must first change belief systems about intelligence, learning and relationships. This entails switching our mindsets from a deficit-based model to one where learners are viewed as capable and unique and where we meet children where they are. Only then can we design an environment where the value of growth outweighs that of test scores. Following in the footsteps of Ross Greene (2014), we must start with the guiding philosophy that "kids do well if they can."

In the Flexible Mindsets model, our interpretation of growth mindsets is incorporated as I CAN messages. These are the messages that we hear from others and say to ourselves that *tell us that our brains can always grow and that we are capable of getting smarter.* A sense of competency is critical for learners as they evolve and become self-determining. It is also mandatory for shifting our practices towards equitable education.

Beyond the growth mindset is a Flexible Mindset. Rather than attributing success primarily to effort, people with Flexible Mindsets focus on the link between ownership of learning, strategy use, perseverance and outcomes.

The construct of growth mindsets allows for approaches that encourage children to be hopeful and persevere. Yet more is required for children to develop successful competencies for today's crises and the uncertainties of the future. In this framework, learning from errors and celebrating what we don't know are critical for success. Mistakes are not viewed as failures, but as opportunities to think critically, solve complex problems and be creative. By reframing mistakes and embracing everything we don't know yet, we tip the scales in a direction that is more equitable.

In a Flexible Mindsets environment, we hear language such as the following:

> "I can see this is tricky for you. When things are tough it means we're learning and getting smarter. What questions do you have that we can use to understand more about this?"

> "This is a new topic, so there is going to be a lot of information we don't know yet and we could get overwhelmed. What part of this topic are you most curious about? Let's explore from there."

Sharing positive instances of the power of Flexible Mindsets allows children to visualise the process of learning from mistakes and persevering. Showcase specific instances of students who have taken on a big challenge, persevered and succeeded. Invite them to share the process of how they got from 'not yet' to 'there'. Evaluate all students relevant to their own progress by meeting them where they are and highlighting the instances where they have shown even incremental growth. Rather than having a set of uniform benchmarks that all children must reach before being acknowledged, education in uncertain times values all indicators of learning.

Never underestimate the value of modelling I CAN messages. Children, in particular, have no idea what teachers and parents are actually thinking. Using talk alouds is essential for making our thoughts explicit. Model how to use opportunities for self-discovery. Explain that you grow and learn from mistakes and struggles. Let your students know that adults have tough days, too, and share with them what you say to yourself to keep you going.

> "I'm feeling tired today and I can tell by the tone in my voice that I'm not being patient. Instead of reacting, I need to remind myself to take a moment to breathe before I respond."

Metacognition and I CAN messages are the foundational steps towards Flexible Mindsets. Flexible Mindsets come to life when we add executive function processes and the flexible use of strategies for learning HOW to learn.

Flexible Mindsets and executive function processes

It is not enough to just be aware of learning-related information and to see oneself as capable of learning. Learners need explicit, direct instruction to develop the tools to manage their own learning. Learners often struggle to learn new strategies unless they have been modelled, talked about explicitly and practised. It is imperative that we teach executive function processes within the context of academic content (Meltzer 2014). Teaching strategies in isolation virtually eliminates the possibility that learners will build the capacity to apply, transfer and adapt strategies in everyday learning situations.

There is considerable debate in the field regarding both the definition and measurement of executive function processes (Meltzer, Dunstan-Brewer & Krishnan 2018). We have listed the definitions of executive function processes as conceptualised by three different well-established experts in the field:

- self-directed actions needed to choose goals and create, enact and sustain actions toward those goals (Barkley 2012);
- the skills needed when we have to think and concentrate, rather than using automatic skills or acting impulsively (Diamond 2016); and
- a collection of interrelated processes responsible for purposeful, goal-directed and flexible behaviour (Meltzer 2014).

Newer theories support the notion that executive function is also involved in toggling between the focused and diffuse modes of learning (Oakley & Sejnowski 2018). A common misconception is that learning only occurs when we are in focused mode, where we are intently concentrating on a problem and trying to find the solution. However, the diffuse mode is essential for Creativity and for solving those problems we have never seen before or are having trouble understanding. When we 'sleep on' an idea or shift to a different activity, it allows the kinds of associative thinking where we can jump from idea to idea and make new connections.

In the Flexible Mindsets model, *executive function processes are: what we use when we identify a goal, when we use what we know to figure out what to do, and make it happen* (see Figure 1.3). They are the mental workstation and playground from which the 3C's (Critical Thinking, Complex Problem-Solving and Creativity) spring. They

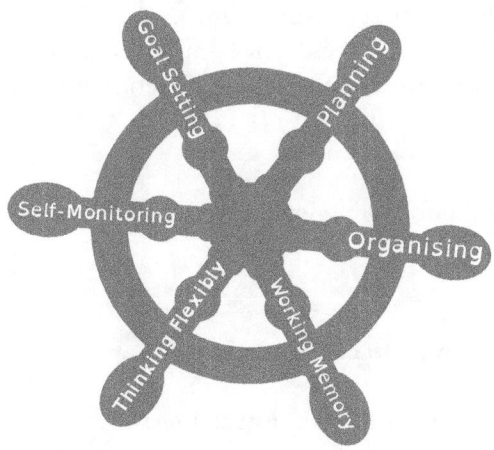

Figure 1.3 Key executive function processes

activate the struggle and deeper exploration required for self-directed learning. They help us ask and answer the questions: *Does this make sense? What else can we try? What are the possibilities?*

Given the familiarity that most educators have with three foundational processes, we briefly provide our definitions. This will be followed by a more in-depth discussion about working memory, cognitive flexibility and self-monitoring, those executive function processes most highlighted by researchers (Diamond 2016; Center on the Developing Child at Harvard University 2011).

Goal setting and initiating: We can't achieve anything if we don't know what we want to do. Purpose is the drive that gives our lives meaning. It is long-lasting and durable (Damon 2009). Once you know what you want to do, it is much easier to initiate a task, be purposeful and see the process through to completion. Many of the challenges to getting started on a task can be addressed by starting with the end in mind, breaking goals down into manageable chunks (subgoals) and using mental imagery. A mental anchor can be formed to visualise where we are going and how we are going to get there (Barkley 2012; Ward & Jacobson 2014). In the Flexible Mindsets model, *goal setting and initiating is knowing what you want to do and turning your mind's eye towards that purpose.*

Planning and prioritising: Planning is the ability to think about the future and figure out what you need to do to reach your goals. It answers the question "What steps can I take to get there?" Unlike chunking a goal into subgoals, planning is: *identifying the steps to reach a goal, recording those steps visually and estimating the time each step will take*. It is inseparable from prioritisation, which is deciding how important tasks are and how urgently they need to get done.

Organising: Organising is *making sense of and ordering materials and ideas into a cohesive whole for the purpose of working towards a goal.* The sifting and sorting of materials and ideas is an individualised process (Meltzer 2010). Success is about developing a system that makes it easier to retrieve information from the brain. Each learner needs to find a format that helps them make sense of their ideas (e.g., outlines, mind maps, graphic organisers, storyboards).

Having briefly reviewed these three foundational processes, we now present three additional research-driven executive function processes.

Working memory

In your head, put the following letters in alphabetical order:

Q L G V K

What did you have to do to complete this task?

- understand and remember the instructions;
- retrieve what you already know (the sequence of the alphabet);

- reorder the letters;
- keep track of where you are in the process;
- hold on to all of these things until you have solved the problem;

Working memory is the mental workspace where we hold and manipulate information in order to: store it in long-term memory; solve problems; and produce output (see Figure 1.4). It is critical for making sense of events that unfold over time (Diamond 2016; Ward & Jacobsen 2014). Working memory allows us to follow instructions and juggle the demands of complex tasks such as written expression (Meltzer 2014). In working memory, we are continually relating bits of information to each other and making connections that are ongoing in pursuit of a goal.

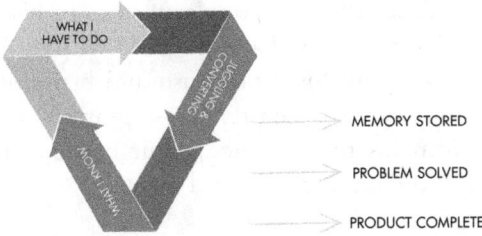

Figure 1.4 Working memory in action

Working memory has a limited capacity and presents unavoidable challenges in every classroom. We can't force working memory capacity to get bigger. Yet there are two things we can do to support working memory:

1. teach strategies that facilitate working memory such as using self-talk and/or gestures to help us picture if-then thinking;
2. reduce the load on working memory. For example, when a student sits down for a math test and immediately writes down the mnemonic for long division.

Zahir had a problem that he shared during his coaching session. He struggled to remember everything he needed to do to get ready for school in the morning. He was tired of his mom nagging him the whole time. He wanted to get ready on his own, but the visual schedule and checklists his mom had made didn't help him. He would start off looking at the list of things he needed to do that was posted on the mirror in his bedroom, but then he would get distracted and the list would be in a different room and he would get lost in a game or a television show and completely lose track of what he was supposed to be doing. He reported that his only reminders would be his mom yelling at him to do ten things all at once. Even though his routine was virtually the same every morning, Zahir said he found it hard to remember everything on the list.

We practised using the strategy of visualizing his future self (Ward & Jacobsen 2014). He practised picturing himself completing his morning routine and, most importantly, what he would look like when he was ready for school. This created a mental anchor that helped him to get back on track when he got distracted, without being dependent on his mom to prompt the next step or constantly give him reminders. We met with his mom to review the strategy and ask for assistance with implementing it at home. His mom took a picture of Zahir standing at the front door with everything he needs to be ready for school (i.e., dressed in uniform, backpack and lunchbox). This became his mental anchor that he refers to when he gets off track. Then his mother did a picture/gesture walk of the first couple of steps in his routine with him each morning. Zahir pictured himself and gestured with his index finger walking to the bathroom, picking up his toothbrush and brushing his teeth. They both agreed to give this a try with the first two steps until he could do them without any reminders from his mom. Once Zahir became independent with these steps, they would add another step, and so on.

Thinking flexibly

In the Flexible Mindsets model, we use the symbol of a helm to highlight the pivotal role of *Thinking Flexibly, the learner's dexterity in shifting perspectives and changing course*. In everyday contexts, we often think of phrases like: *handling curve balls, making lemonade out of lemons, walking in someone else's shoes, shifting gears, not seeing the forest for the trees* and *thinking on your feet*. These are good examples of instances where we need to modify strategies; however, thinking flexibly is required for a much broader scope of our everyday functioning. Thinking flexibly requires us to:

- understand the perspectives of others (especially those that differ from our own);
- interpret language that has multiple meanings;
- shift constantly between the different phases in a process;
- shift back and forth between a main idea and details;
- visualise multiple outcomes; and
- evaluate the effectiveness of a strategy and, if necessary, adapt that strategy or shift to another approach.

The capacity of imagining possible futures to reach a goal occurs in what Russell Barkley calls "the mind's playground" (Barkley 2014a, p. 3). This notion illustrates the collective value of shoring up working memory space, thinking flexibly and then being able to evaluate and implement potential solutions.

Miya had to read a long and complex chapter in her history textbook in preparation for writing an essay about the Industrial Revolution. She had read the first few pages, but when she came to her coaching session, she reported that she couldn't really remember anything she had read and that it wasn't really making any sense. I asked Miya if she was aware of the difference between the main idea versus the details and she informed me that she knew the difference, but she didn't understand what it had to do with reading a chapter in a textbook.

I showed Miya how a chapter in a book is typically structured with subheadings, topic sentences and supporting details. We deconstructed a few paragraphs together and picked out the main ideas and details. Once Miya started to be able to identify these on her own, I explained how to use this strategy of shifting between the main idea and details to help her comprehension and note taking. We talked about how note taking can be used as a retrieval practice strategy by turning headings and subheadings into questions for quizzing yourself. She practised creating an outline of the chapter by shifting between the main themes and details and turning that information into questions. At the end of the chapter, she reviewed her outline and she could see how all the pieces fit together to communicate the central idea of the chapter. Later we applied this same strategy of identifying the structure of the information to create an outline for her essay.

Self-monitoring

Most definitions of monitoring refer to the ability to follow your progress during tasks to make sure you stay on track. Keeping on track means monitoring your thoughts, the strategies you are using and your progress towards a goal. When we don't give this process our full attention, it's easy to slip into autopilot, causing us to miss important details, fall back on assumptions and make impulsive errors. Our thoughts end up looking like a snow globe. Our brains become a 'blizzard of ideas', with lots of flakes swirling around our heads and no coherent organisation. If we keep shaking the snow globe, we can't think clearly (Bertin 2018).

Stilling the snow globe requires moment to moment attention where we are learning to catch our thoughts and notice when we are off task. It happens when we are able to observe our thoughts and suspend judgement. Noticing helps us settle under stress, find clarity and recognise whether or not we are on track. This is the evaluative part of self-monitoring.

In the Flexible Mindsets model, self-monitoring means so much more than tracking progress during a task and checking over our work. Once we have evaluated our learning, we need to calibrate. When we notice that we are not effectively working towards our goals, this is one of those metacognitive 'Uh oh!' experiences alerting us that we need to do something differently. This is when we need to put the brakes on. A pause gives us a chance to reflect and respond, instead of just reacting. We need to take the temperature of our emotions. Are we overly alert or not alert enough? How can we adjust our emotions for our brains to be optimally ready for learning? This is our chance to reframe any negative mindset messages using constructive self-talk. From a more balanced emotional state, we are ready to examine where we have gone off track and redirect our attention to that piece in the process. What isn't working? What else can I try? We can use hindsight to figure out what did and didn't work in the past. This is where self-monitoring and thinking flexibly are interwoven. This is calibration; when we regulate our feelings, mental energy and strategies.

In the Flexible Mindsets model, *self-monitoring is when you* EVALUATE *your learning and* CALIBRATE *your actions.* It gives you ownership of your learning and puts you in the driver's seat. As Russell Barkley asks:

Can you stop? Can you wait? . . . You must build in a pause between an event and what you plan to do about it.

(Barkley 2014b)

Samuel had difficulty focusing during class. He knew he was often bored in class and tended to daydream. His teachers commented frequently that he needed to pay attention more and it was always mentioned in his report card. He tried telling himself to focus more, but that never seemed to work. This had been going on for so long that he just figured there was nothing he could do about it. During one of our sessions early in the school year, I asked Samuel if there was anything he thought he could work on that would make a difference for him at school. He said he thought that if he could just figure out how to pay attention more in class, his grades would improve.

I explained that one of the things that was making it hard for Samuel to 'just focus more' was that in order to spend more time on task, you first need to notice when you are distracted. We started by brainstorming all the things that distract him. He then chose one distraction – other students talking in class – and agreed to notice and make a tally mark in his planner every time he found himself distracted by other people talking. When we reviewed his tally marks the next week, he was amazed at how many times he got distracted, but he was even more amazed that he actually noticed. It was the first time Samuel realised he had some control over his thoughts and he was excited to try a strategy to get back on task. After reviewing a list of strategies that he could try when he noticed he was distracted, he decided he wanted to start with self-talk. When he noticed he was distracted, he would ask himself, "What should I be doing right now?" After spending more time noticing when he was distracted and trying different strategies, he found that using specific strategies to participate more in class was one of his most effective tools. Several of his teachers even commented in his midterm report card that they noticed he was participating more. When we reviewed his report card together in our session, Samuel's face lit up when I pointed out how many teachers had noticed his increased participation. He was beginning to feel more in control of his learning and proud of what he was able to do on his own.

The journey of self-directed learning

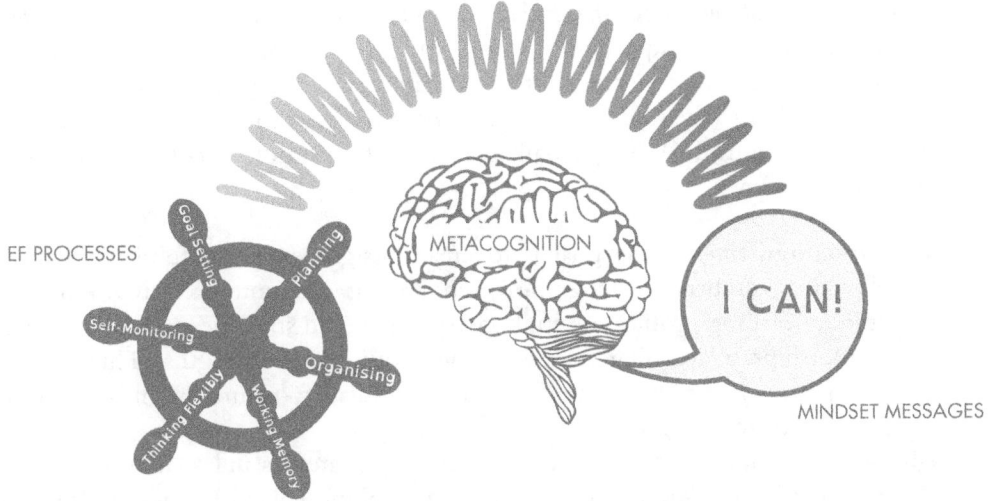

Figure 1.5 The Flexible Mindsets model

What happens when we fuse metacognition, I CAN mindset messages and executive function processes? We create an environment and culture where learners are aware of 'What Works When', believe that they are capable and actively apply the tools they need to learn HOW to learn (see Figure 1.5). *A Flexible Mindset is the dynamic and ongoing interaction between self-awareness, adaptive strategy use and perseverance that empower learners to evolve and become self-directed.*

The Flexible Mindsets Spiral of Reflective Learning: get started with Flexible Mindsets

In our work, we have developed a system for transforming mindsets in schools. We call this the Flexible Learning Environmental Scan (FLES) and it comprises three original tools.

- Firstly, as a leader, you can raise your own self-awareness and change your own mindset by engaging with the Flexible Mindsets Spiral of Reflective Learning as presented next. (See also the end of Chapters 1, 2, 3, 4 and 5 and Appendix A).
- Next, you can use our Metacognitive Insights Survey (MIS) to help your students take the initial steps to reflect on their strengths and weaknesses in reference to the 3C's (see the end of Chapters 6, 7 and 8 and also Appendix B).
- As your classroom is transformed, you can use the Flexible Learning Activation Checklist (FLAC) to track progress (see the end of Chapters 6, 7 and 8 and also Appendix C).

The Flexible Mindsets Spiral of Reflective Learning is an ongoing process that educators can use to raise self-awareness and change their mindsets alongside those of their students. This dynamic process ultimately transforms classrooms into environments that are makers of self-directed learners. More importantly, by encouraging students to parallel this process in their own learning, we can shift the balance of the responsibility for learning from the teacher to the student and from what they need to know to learning HOW to learn (see Figure 1.6). The five phases we use to promote self-directed learning are listed as follows.

- **Be metacognitive** – The goal is to create assignments that fulfil curriculum objectives, embed metacognition and present a counternarrative. Consider unique learning profiles, multiple perspectives and strategies to work towards partnerships in learning that turn the spotlight on strengths. Think about learning objectives from the curriculum to identify natural points of convergence with teaching self-awareness.
- **Model** – Learners often struggle to learn new strategies unless they have been modelled and talked about explicitly. 'Talk alouds' allow learners to 'see' the mental processes that others use to describe their unique brains and how they learn best.
- **Ask questions and afford time** – Deeper thinking develops through a process where a learner is allowed to struggle. Turn instructions into tools by unpacking terms such as *think about it, focus, explain, reason, analyse* (Warshauer 2015). Know each child and tailor your responses to strike a balance between not jumping in to rescue and not leaving a student to flounder past the point of frustration. This is what ultimately builds autonomy.
- **Use sharing as a springboard** – By sharing strategies overtly, students can begin to reflect on 'What Works When'. Find opportunities to ask students to share what they are doing, what works and what isn't working to reach a goal. Showcase the contributions from students who grapple and are comfortable expressing what they don't know.
- **Think on your feet** – Being responsive to students involves meeting them where they are and building on this common ground. This requires planning in the

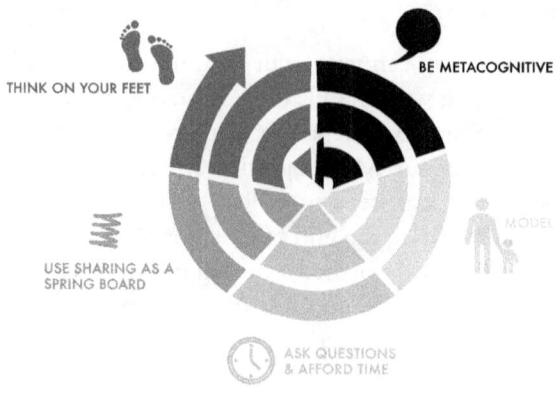

Figure 1.6 The Flexible Mindsets Spiral of Reflective Learning

moment, using knowledge about your students' strengths and challenges and being in tune with their emotional states. It also means a constant awareness of how your responses may inadvertently reinforce fixed mentalities. Abandon knee-jerk reactions in favour of thoughtful responses.

As applied to the concepts from this chapter, you can get started with the Spiral of Reflective Learning with the ideas in Table 1.1.

Table 1.1 The Flexible Mindsets Spiral of Reflective Learning: get started with Flexible Mindsets

 **BE METACOGNITIVE**	How will you help your students understand the importance of metacognition (awareness of thinking and learning) and gain deeper insights into their use of strategies? How can you make metacognition visible in your classroom?
 **MODEL**	Think of a problem you recently solved. How could you model Flexible Mindsets by sharing the multiple ways you could have solved it and why you chose your final solution? "I kept losing my phone. My friends made many suggestions such as having someone call my phone, using the 'find my phone app' and always putting my phone in my pocket. In the end, I decided that the best solution was to pair my phone with something I would always take with me, so I bought a wallet that has a phone pocket in it."
 **ASK QUESTIONS AND AFFORD TIME**	What questions am I using that afford students time to delve deeper into concepts? What questions can I use to shift the balance of instruction to give students more ownership over their learning? Instead of starting a lesson by telling students what they have learned previously, ask students "Let's connect today's lesson with yesterday's. What are the main points from yesterday's lesson? What do you think we are going to talk about today?"
 **USE SHARING AS A SPRINGBOARD**	Think of a recent assignment you have given or test you have scored. How will you encourage students to share the strategies they used and then highlight that different strategies work better for some people than others? After handing back a test, ask, "Look at your grade and think of the tools you used to study. Does your grade match what you would expect based on how you studied? What tools worked and didn't work?"
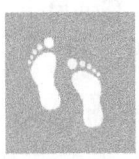 **THINK ON YOUR FEET**	Keep a log of times when class activities don't go according to plan. What do you see happening when class discussions stay on track versus when they go off track?

References

Barkley, R. (2012). *Executive functions: What they are, how they work, and why they evolved.* New York, NY: Guilford.

Barkley, R. (2014a). *ADHD & the mind's playground: Uncut with Dr. Russell Barkley.* Hamilton, ON: Big Brain Productions.

Barkley, R. (2014b). 30 Essential ideas you should know about ADHD, 3A the five executive functions [online]. *YouTube.* [Viewed 26 April 2017]. Available from: www.youtube.com/watch?v=Illf_Hsy570

Baron-Cohen, S. (1995). *Mindblindness: An essay on autism and theory of mind.* Cambridge, MA: MIT Press.

Beckett, B. (2006). *Genesis.* New York, NY: Houghton Mifflin Harcourt.

Bertin, M. (2018). *How children thrive: The practical science of raising independent, resilient, and happy kids.* Boulder, CO: Sounds True.

Brooks, R. (2015). *Resilience: The common underlying factor.* [online]. 14 April 2015. [Viewed 15 August 2020]. Available from: www.drrobertbrooks.com/resilience-common-underlying-factor/

Brooks, R., & Goldstein, S. (2002). *Raising resilient children: Fostering strength, hope, and optimism in your child.* New York, NY: McGraw Hill.

Center on the Developing Child at Harvard University. (2011). *Building the brain's "Air Traffic Control" system: How early experiences shape the development of executive function.* Working Paper No. 11. Available from: https://developingchild.harvard.edu/wp-content/uploads/2011/05/How-Early-Experiences-Shape-the-Development-of-Executive-Function.pdf

Damon, W. (2009). *The path to purpose: How young people find their calling in life.* New York, NY: Free Press.

Diamond, A. (2016). Why improving and assessing executive functions early in life is critical. In: J. Griffin, P. McCardle, & L. Freund, eds. *Executive function in preschool-age children: Integrating measurement, neurodevelopment, and translational research.* Washington, DC: American Psychological Association. pp. 11–44.

Dweck, C. (2008). *Mindset: The new psychology of success.* New York, NY: Ballantine.

Flavell, J. (1981). Cognitive monitoring. In: W. Dickson, ed. *Children's oral communication.* New York, NY: Academic Press. pp. 35–60.

Flavell, J. (2000). Development of children's knowledge about the mental world. *International Journal of Behavioral Development.* **24**, 15–23.

Goldstein, S., & Brooks, R. (2013). Why study resilience? In: S. Goldstein & R. Brooks, eds. *Handbook of resilience in children.* 2nd ed. New York, NY: Springer. pp. 3–14.

Grant, A. (2021). *Think again: The power of knowing what you don't know.* New York, NY: Viking.

Greene, R. (2014). *Lost at school: Why our kids with behavioral challenges are falling through the cracks and how we can help them.* New York, NY: Scribner.

Gweon, H., & Saxe, R. (2013). Developmental cognitive neuroscience of Theory of Mind. In: J. Rubenstein & P. Rakic, eds. *Neural circuit development and function in the brain: Comprehensive developmental neuroscience.* Cambridge, MA: Academic Press. pp. 367–377.

Meltzer, L. (2010). *Promoting executive function in the classroom.* New York, NY: Guilford Press.

Meltzer, L. (2014). Teaching executive function processes: Promoting metacognition, strategy use, and effort. In: S. Goldstein & J. Naglieri, eds. *Executive functioning handbook.* New York, NY: Springer-Verlag. pp. 445–474.

Meltzer, L., Dunstan-Brewer, J., & Krishnan, K. (2018). Learning differences and executive function: Understandings and misunderstandings. In: L. Meltzer, ed. *Executive function in education: From theory to practice.* 2nd ed. New York, NY: Guilford Press. pp. 109–141.

National Scientific Council on the Developing Child. (2015). *Supportive relationships and active skill-building strengthen the foundations of resilience.* Working Paper No. 13. Available from: https://developingchild.harvard.edu/resources/supportive-relationships-and-active-skill-building-strengthen-the-foundations-of-resilience/

Oakley, B., & Sejnowski, T. (2018). *Learning how to learn: How to succeed in school without spending all your time studying.* New York, NY: Penguin Random House.

Premack, D., & Woodruff, G. (1978). Does the chimpanzee have a theory of mind? *Behavioral and Brain Sciences.* **1**(4), 515–526.

Ryan, R., & Deci, E. (2017). *Self-determination theory: Basic psychological needs in motivation, development, and wellness.* New York, NY: Guilford Press.

Sweetland, D., & Stolberg, R. (2015). *Teaching kids to think: Raising confident, independent, and thoughtful children in an age of instant gratification.* Naperville, IL: Sourcebooks.

Taylor, S. (1999). Better learning through better thinking: Developing students' metacognitive abilities. *Journal of College Reading and Learning.* **30**(1), 34–45.

Ward, S., & Jacobsen, K. (2014). A clinical model for developing executive function skills. *Perspectives on Language Learning and Education.* **21**(2), 72–84.

Warshauer, H. (2015). Productive struggle in middle school mathematics classrooms. *Journal of Mathematics Teacher Education.* **17**(4), 375–400.

Winner, M. (2007). *Thinking about you, thinking about me.* San Jose, CA: Think Social.

CHAPTER 2

What is the mechanism for Flexible Mindsets? Productive Puzzling and curiosity

The thrust of the Flexible Mindsets initiative is to empower people to direct their own learning. Self-directed learners actively focus mental energy on their goals and apply their learning to new and meaningful contexts, even when challenged. To take charge of their own learning, they must be driven by curiosity, a desire to grow and the love of learning. This ability to learn HOW to learn can be deliberately and consciously grown through direct engagement in active learning.

In this chapter, we will introduce the active learning concept of Productive Puzzling: the key mechanism we use to engage learners along the journey of Flexible Mindsets. In the next section of this book, Chapters 3 through 5 will highlight the implications of fixed mentalities and demonstrate how Flexible Mindsets can open the window for learning and provide tools for learning HOW to learn.

Socrates, an ancient Greek philosopher, believed that disciplined practice of thoughtful questioning enabled students to examine ideas logically and to determine the validity of those ideas. Charles Darwin, who illuminated the theory of evolution by natural selection, identified the central role of 'perplexed reflection' in science and learning. The Flexible Mindsets model builds upon these historical thinkers and newer ideas by incorporating recent work in mathematics education on the role of Productive Struggle (Warshauer 2015). In mathematics, Productive Struggle occurs in settings where it is safe to take risks, where students can share their struggle and where wrong answers are not seen as failures but rather opportunities to explore, grow and learn. By extension, *Productive Puzzling is being engrossed in a perplexing problem that is within your grasp but requires thinking, grappling and reasoning*. It is the springboard for Critical Thinking, Complex Problem-Solving and Creativity.

Curiosity is both the foundation of and partner to Productive Puzzling. *To be curious is to be inquisitive about the environment, an event, an object, a process or a concept.* Curiosity drives our desire to investigate and to learn. It is what happens when we encounter something unusual, novel or unexpected and it is marked by questions such as *I wonder what would happen if . . . ? How does this work? What could this be used for?* Productive Puzzling, by definition, must involve a dimension of feeling perplexed, leading us to ask, *Does this make sense? What else could we try? What are the possibilities?*

> In this chapter, we will:
>
> - explain why curiosity is important for deeper thinking and learning;
> - provide straightforward information about what happens in the brain when we are curious; and
> - introduce the five conditions that are necessary for Productive Puzzling.

Why is curiosity so important for deeper thinking and learning?

Eating in a diner one day, I overheard a conversation between four college students. There was a 'machine' next to their table and one student said, "What's that?" The four friends then engaged in a collaborative process of examining parts of the object and discussing what each piece actually did. One student inferred that the titles listed along each row were songs from "the 70's – a long time ago." Eventually, the group concluded that you put coins in the slot, press a button that corresponds to a particular song and then that song is played by the device. They were satisfied with their answer and moved on to other topics of conversation. I thought to myself: I wonder what would have happened, if, when they first asked the question, I had leaned across and said, "It's a juke box."

Curiosity is just as important as IQ in determining how well students do in school and beyond. When curious, learners persevere, study and remember more. They read at a more meaningful level and attain higher grades (Silvia 2008). Curious students not only ask more questions and deeper questions, but they are also more active in seeking the answers. Without curiosity, would artist Kareem Abdul Jabbar have had success in such a wide variety of endeavours, from athleticism to film to authorship to global cultural advocacy? Would mathematician Grace Topper have been a pioneer in the field of technology and earned the National Medal of Technology and the Presidential Medal of Freedom? Would explorer Mae Jemison have evolved from a Peace Corps medical officer to become the first female African American astronaut, a founder of a nonprofit, an author and a science ambassador?

By motivating people to learn for its own sake, curiosity ensures that people will develop a broad set of knowledge, skills and experiences. When interested, students persist longer at learning tasks, spend more time studying, read more deeply, remember more of what they read and get better grades in their classes (Silvia 2008). People seem to understand that curiosity enhances their motivation and performance. When faced with a boring task, people will use strategies to make it more interesting, such as working with a friend or making the task more complex (Sansone & Thoman 2005). Curiosity is the motivation for active learning.

What happens in the brain when we puzzle?

Trying new things has an adaptive function that has been critical for human evolution. Unfamiliar things often signal something dangerous or harmful. What we learn from new experiences can help us to respond effectively to unexpected circumstances and to counterbalance feelings of uncertainty and anxiety (Kashdan 2004).

The brain is wired for the survival functions of surveillance and alert. Curiosity is a response that activates the brain's arousal network. If the system detects something unusual, it can sound an alarm that is heard brain wide and this is when intrinsic alertness transforms into phasic alertness (Peterson & Posner 2012). Anything that is novel, unusual, unpredictable or distinctive puts our brains on alert and therefore our brains are wired to pay closer attention to them (Medina 2008).

In a recent research study, participants rated how curious they were to learn the answers to more than 100 trivia questions. The researchers then used fMRI scans to see what was happening in the brain when participants felt especially curious about the answer to a question (Gruber, Gelman & Ranganath 2014). The results revealed that curiosity prepares the brain for learning by acting like a vortex. The resulting void causes us to seek out stimulation. Thus curiosity puts the brain in a state that allows it to learn and retain new information. The implication of this is that if a teacher can arouse students' curiosity, they will be more engaged in learning. Another key finding from this research study is that curiosity can make learning a more rewarding experience for students. Researchers found that when curiosity had been sparked, there was increased brain activity in the hippocampus, which is involved in creating memories as well as the circuitry related to reward and pleasure. When these circuits are aroused, dopamine – the 'feel good' chemical in our brain – is released. So, piquing students' curiosity can help them remember lessons and make their learning experiences pleasurable.

Educators have long recognised that students learn better when new material is linked to prior knowledge. Existing knowledge, concepts and systems are easier to process than novel material. Activating this base makes it easier to grapple with more difficult cognitive work. There is no thinking without knowing (Willingham 2009). There is no meaningful learning without active engagement.

Based on evolutionary theories, scientists can now better explain how our brains are wired to pay attention to information connected to existing memories (Medina 2008). Our 10,000-year old brains were not designed for the world we live in today. They were built when we walked or ran many miles a day. This is why our brains crave exercise and we get a brain boost when we get up and move. Our brains are designed to process visual information quickly and can pay attention for about ten minutes. This adaptive function is rooted in evolution. Humans who failed to instantaneously attend to threatening situations did not live long enough to pass on their genes. Thus, we are programmed to use our previous experiences to accurately remember threatening situations and to direct *where* we pay attention.

Thinking, on the other hand, is slow and effortful and our brains are not built for it. It is not efficient and reliable to think. Thinking is hard work so it is not surprising that people have to really motivate themselves to engage in it.

Thinking was not evolutionarily helpful (see Figure 2.1). Stop and think and you might end up . . .

Figure 2.1 The evolutionary value of NOT thinking

So much of our brain's real estate is taken up by activities related to seeing and moving. Our brains are not wired to think in the ways that are demanded of us in traditional classroom settings. They are naturally curious and designed to scan the environment, explore and alert us to threats. We are powerful and natural explorers (Medina 2008).

Educational practices are not aligned with what we now know about brain development. We are expecting students to exert mental effort for several hours during the school day and then go home and do hours of homework, leaving no time for processing, reflecting, integrating and connecting. When made to perform on traditional school-based tasks, our brains are being asked to do things that run contrary to their evolutionary purpose. Since thinking is such hard work, and does not provide rewards that stimulate dopamine release, children rarely experience joy in academic learning. If we want students to be motivated to engage in thinking, we need to convince them that their mental work will be worth it.

One effective way to do this is to use curiosity to engage learners in exploration, invention and improvisation. We all weigh the potential pleasure of solving a problem against the mental effort required. If the challenge is too difficult or too easy, our brains disengage from the process. If the recipe is perfectly balanced, we are tapping into curiosity and ensuring that students enjoy thinking and learning (Willingham 2009).

The potential to pique curiosity lies in experiences that are emotionally laden and meaningful (Medina 2008). Incongruity is particularly effective for engaging our brains. If you want learners to become engaged and ask questions, present something that is unexpected, odd, absurd, juxtaposed or humorous.

Guidelines for piquing curiosity

1 Consider that content and delivery matter

A group of students attends a field trip to the science museum, specifically to watch the IMAX film celebrating the 50th anniversary of Apollo 11. This documentary film uses original footage to describe the 1969 Apollo 11 mission, the first spaceflight in which men walked on the Moon. Ciana is an explorer by nature: she loves science, especially astronomy, and has a precise replica of the solar system on the ceiling of her bedroom. Esther, on the other hand, is an artist: she writes beautiful poetry and loves epic shows such as *Star Trek: Discovery*. The factual style and technical information in *Apollo 11* fuse naturally with Ciana's preexisting scientific knowledge and her head is buzzing with new questions and ideas about future possibilities. Esther has an entirely different experience. She comprehends very little about basic concepts such as gravity and acceleration and can't access most of the material. The dry style of presentation does nothing to grab her attention and her imagination is stifled.

There are aspects of thinking we enjoy because we get a sense of pleasure from finding solutions (solving problems). There are also lots of things that require thinking that we would never choose to do and many others that would simply bore us. While the type of content matters – we are more curious about things that interest us – the delivery of the content is what matters most when it comes to piquing curiosity. When content is presented through a medium we enjoy, is connected to a story or includes an element of surprise, even the most boring topic can spur our curiosity (Willingham 2009).

2 Remember inspiration can't be forced

Salvador Dali, a 20th-century surrealist painter, used to sit in a chair with keys in his hand along with an upside down plate on the floor and let his mind wander until he fell asleep. His hand would release the keys as soon as he slipped into a deeper state of sleep and the sound of the keys clinking on a metal plate would wake him up. This little amount of rest is just enough to awaken creativity. In this state, his mind brought together distant ideas in a new way. He believed that this process led to some of his best ideas.

Somewhere deep within each of us is an affinity, *something that, when we are in the midst of it, engages us to the point that we don't even notice what is happening around us.* The outside world just disappears. When we are engrossed in an affinity, time moves so quickly that we are unaware that it has passed. All the energy and brain power that we use does not even feel like hard work (Silvia 2006). Inspiration flows from the thinking that we do when our brains are in the diffuse mode. Using the metaphor of a brain as a flashlight, the diffuse mode casts a broad, scattered light whereas the focused mode is concentrated light (Oakley & Sejnowski 2018). Our brains enter the diffuse mode during moments when we are not explicitly thinking, such as when listening to music, exercising, taking a walk, mind-wandering and sleeping (Gkiokas 2018).

In contrast to mindfulness which focuses the brain, mind-wandering allows the brain to be more creative (Zomorodi 2017). Purposeful learning occurs when we shift flexibly between focused thinking and meandering. So, when we need to destress, we meditate; when we want inspiration, we daydream.

3 Make it comprehensible

There are two types of evaluations that learners make when faced with a challenge (Silvia 2005; 2008). One assessment is the level of novelty: the degree to which something is new, unexpected, surprising or intriguing. Decades of research show that new and unexpected events can pique our curiosity (Berlyne 1960). Secondly, we judge whether or not a challenge is comprehensible. We think about our skills, knowledge and resources to deal with an event (Lazarus 1991). If we perceive a goal as incomprehensible, we give up. In the case of curiosity, we are responding to an unexpected situation. If we perceive an event as both new and as comprehensible, curiosity is activated (Silvia 2008). Perceiving something as being comprehensible is the bridge between feeling curious and feeling bored or discouraged. Feeling lost and confused shuts down our learning. Novelty, coupled with the seeds of comprehension, sparks learning.

4 Build in time off-task (to space out)

We often see boredom as a negative state and something to be avoided. Boredom is actually the place we all need to visit as an intermediary between busywork and inspiration. Boredom is a state of mind that happens when we take away distractions such as cell phones, video games and television. It is not enough to simply remove distractions. True boredom happens when we have 'nothing to do' and no one is demanding anything of us. Boredom alerts us that we are no longer pursuing purposeful goals. The current goal is no longer satisfactory, attractive or meaningful (Elpidorou 2014). This leaves us feeling restless, agitated and uncomfortable (Zomorodi 2017) and we crave escape. In order to avoid feeling trapped in an unfulfilling state, we begin searching for something to stimulate us, something that is not readily available in our immediate surroundings. Boredom is both a warning and a push (Elpidorou 2014).

The push of boredom allows us to 'space out'. Our thoughts don't stop just because there is nothing to do with those thoughts. It may appear that the brain is shutting down; it is actually digging into a vast trove of memories, imagining future possibilities, dissecting our interactions with other people and reflecting on who we are. "It feels like we're wasting time when we wait for the longest red light in the world to turn green, but the brain is putting ideas and events into perspective" (Zomorodi 2017, p. 21).

Boredom is necessary.

5 Let it be. Don't give the answer

When babies learn to sit up and crawl, they cannot yet walk. Would we carry all babies everywhere with us, rather than watch them repeatedly try to stand up and fall over? How heavy would they get before we decided they were too heavy to carry around? Would it then be *too late* for them to learn how to walk?

Make it comfortable for learners to stop and think. Adults who want to help often do things for a child which can feed into 'I can't' self-perceptions. Try to wait before jumping in, even if it feels uncomfortable. It takes lots of practice to learn to find the perfectly balanced moment to intervene: after allowing time for experiencing challenge, but before a child has become discouraged.

Some traditional approaches to education involve three steps in learning: watching a model, being assisted and then doing it on your own. These approaches are effective for a range of learning experiences. What they don't do is spark curiosity. They are too predictable and we already know what's going to happen. Developmentally, children also need time and space to explore, make mistakes and struggle. Without struggle, children don't get to experience the benefits of hard work. They may have started out feeling curious, but if we hand them the answers, then a task appears to be too easy and no longer captures their curiosity. This reinforces beliefs that everything must come to us instantaneously and that struggle is not worthwhile. We must avoid cheating students of feeling capable and learning how to do things on their own.

The brain needs to pause to give time for the prefrontal cortex to kick in. This helps us to think and respond, instead of just reacting. Allowing children time to struggle forces them to question, plan, solve problems, organise and grapple with concepts. The more opportunities we give them to tackle appropriately challenging work, the more likely they will be to develop the neural networks to solve future problems.

Adults need to be okay with waiting and suspend the instinct to jump in and rescue children with the answers. We have to be able to observe children's confusion, frustration and discouragement. However, 'letting it be' doesn't mean we should just do nothing. Figuring out when to intervene requires us to take into account the nature of the task, a child's skill set for solving similar problems and the child's tolerance for frustration. When you do intervene, don't do it for them. Rein in your impulse to fix things. Let them know you are there to support them by asking questions such as, "How can I help? Tell me about ____. What have you tried so far? *What else could you try?*"

As Willingham observes, "People are naturally curious, but we are not naturally good thinkers; unless the cognitive conditions are right, we will avoid thinking" (2009, p. 9). In other words, if we always hand out the answer, curiosity will disappear, and with it, Critical Thinking, Complex Problem-Solving and Creativity.

When you think about school, what typically comes to mind? Your own experiences when you were in school? Your children's experiences? Perhaps a particular subject you found fascinating or one that was incredibly boring? The image that comes into my mind is everyday brains doing everyday things. Much of this consists of content download, where students wait to have the teacher tell them what to do or what to think. This type of concrete knowledge is important as the basis for learning, but it is not enough.

Beyond concrete learning, effective teachers find creative ways to pique curiosity. They may use novelty to introduce a topic, present problems that are intriguing and design projects that expand our understanding of the world. They may also use predictions to build anticipation and hook learners into wanting to know more. The simple act of starting a lesson with a question such as "What did we learn yesterday?" instead of providing a summary of the previous lesson can make a significant difference (Agarwal & Bain 2019). These instances achieve the goal of opening up neural pathways for learning. Without further intervention, most brains tend to revert to a more passive state of simply trying to absorb information. Piquing curiosity activates the arousal network and signals potential pleasure in the brain. It allows learners to reach a stage where they are becoming increasingly self-directed, where they can say "get out of my way, but not too far" (Heick 2019). Ultimately, self-reflection empowers learners to effect qualitative changes in their own thinking. Piquing curiosity gets the brain ready for Productive Puzzling and puzzling feeds curiosity.

What are the necessary conditions for Productive Puzzling?

Learning activities that promote Productive Puzzling require five conditions (see Figure 2.2). The foundation must be firmly established by designing an environment that builds trusting relationships and encourages taking risks for learning. The second and third conditions operate interdependently: sufficient challenge to spark curiosity, coupled with solutions that are within reach. Ideally, puzzling is set up to ensure that there are multiple strategies for the solution and, preferably, more than one possible outcome. Opportunities for reflection are built into the process and facilitated after the completion of the activity.

Flexible Mindsets

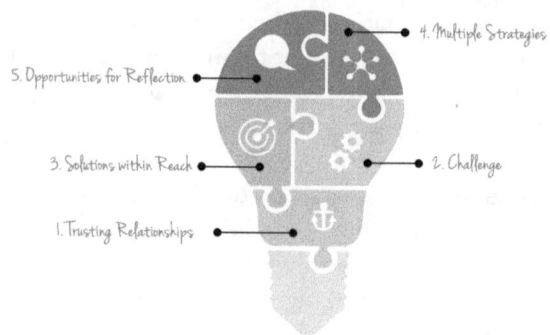

Figure 2.2 The five conditions for Productive Puzzling

Condition 1: trusting relationships for risk-taking

Trust arises from a number of factors within a given environment as well as the actions and reactions of other people. To summarise briefly, it is important to:

- set up physical spaces that invite exploration and co-creation;
- share that the cornerstone of learning is identifying what we don't know and grappling with it;
- clarify that our brains learn best through mistakes and trial and error;
- model the value of mistakes by 'talking aloud' through our own errors;
- celebrate mistakes and their role in creativity, innovation and inventions;
- communicate in ways that build trusting relationships; and
- explicitly troubleshoot challenges and obstacles.

Chapter 4 provides more detail on how to open the window for learning and build trusting relationships for students to ask questions, make mistakes and take risks for learning.

Conditions 2 and 3: challenge and solutions within reach

Having created an environment characterised by trust, we can then begin to introduce conceptual challenges to learners (see Figure 2.3).

A challenge is something difficult that requires mental effort and determination. It is the gap between what is already known and what is yet to be learned. People tend to seek out novelty, but we quickly discard problems that are too easy or too difficult (Willingham 2009). If we start a Sudoku puzzle and solve it quickly and easily, we won't be interested in another puzzle at the same level of difficulty. Conversely, if we can't even figure out the first few numbers, then we will become frustrated and give up.

Figure 2.3 Productive Puzzling balances challenge with solutions that are within reach

As we strive to change the mindsets of students, we place increasing emphasis on the role of challenge for making brains smarter. Setting goals that are both challenging and achievable is largely a matter of structuring tasks in advance. It is crafted from an educator's expertise in concert with relationships that build on the knowledge of individual students. Having set up a challenging puzzle for students, the role of the adult is to facilitate deeper puzzling. We express our confidence in learners to solve puzzles by affording them time in which to ponder and by providing specific guiding questions to promote perseverance and flexible strategy use. Effective interventions focus on breaking a puzzle down into smaller, manageable chunks; encouraging learners to ask questions and explain their thinking; and using their responses to guide the type of open-ended questions you ask next.

Condition 4: multiple strategies

There is more than one trail to the top of the mountain.

Given the pressures of current-day curricula, speed and accuracy in producing the correct answers are highly valued. There is little time for children to explore and figure things out. IQ tests, which are supposed to measure intelligence, rely heavily on already knowing the right answers and on timed responses. Children who take the time to reason and try different strategies to figure out answers are penalised, often resulting in lower scores than children who are less reflective. We inadvertently reinforce the misconception that knowing is superior to not knowing by only showing excitement and pride in students when they give us the right answers. What would it look like and sound like in classrooms all over the world if teachers gave students a high five every time they identified something they didn't know?

A Flexible Mindset is characterised by the ability to try something out, figure out what works and what doesn't and then say: *Does this make sense? What else can we try? What are the possibilities?*

These questions encapsulate the ability to shift perspectives and adapt flexibly when learning. Using open-ended prompts and sharing ideas is critical for assisting learners to recognise that there are multiple ways to reason, many strategies that can lead to a solution and endless possibilities for what something can become.

When learners shift flexibly, they are comfortable with 'not knowing' (Duckworth 2006). They take time to generate and evaluate multiple strategies (Meltzer 2010). It is rare that educational practices include direct instruction highlighting the value of different thoughts and strategies. Before selecting puzzles that can be solved using multiple strategies, set the climate in the classroom by building trusting relationships. Ensure that learners feel secure with the sharing of differing thoughts.

Condition 5: opportunities for reflection

During Productive Puzzling, children initially are engaged in reflection when they are asked to think about the process. However, the greatest opportunities for reflection often happen at the end of an activity or lesson. Metacognition and reflection work hand in hand. As learners become increasingly self-aware, they are better able to reflect upon 'What Works When'. Direct strategy instruction has been proven to improve how students transfer learning, use knowledge creatively and reflect on processes (Meltzer 2013). Strategies such as retrieval practice help students to identify what they do and do not know and focus on deepening their understanding (Agarwal & Bain 2019).

Students need to 'go deep' in reflecting upon their strengths and challenges, as well as the strategies that work best in a given situation. Predicting how they would approach something differently in the future is critical for self-directed learning. Once students have begun to understand and use the language of self-reflection, dialogue in the classroom can explore puzzles at greater depths.

To stoke Productive Puzzling, students must learn to ask and answer the kinds of questions that deepen exploration beyond initial curiosity (see 'Carefully Crafted Questions' in Chapter 5). Adults are charged with teaching students the language of learning: how to think, listen and speak in ways that facilitate deeper learning (Wilson 2015).

Productive Puzzling is the underlying mechanism for Flexible Mindsets. This chapter has defined the five conditions necessary for Productive Puzzling. Applying these principles consistently through the Flexible Mindsets Spiral of Reflective Learning allows educators to take charge in their own classrooms (see Table 2.1). These practices create a culture where students feel comfortable taking learning-related risks, use strategies flexibly and persevere when challenged. Noticing the incongruous, the unexpected, the unfamiliar and the things that provoke a feeling of discomfort entices us to delve further and sets us on course for developing agency in our own learning.

In the next section, Chapter 3 will elaborate on the implications of fixed mentalities in closing the window for learning. Chapter 4 will set the foundation by exploring ways to build trusting relationships so students feel comfortable asking questions, making mistakes and taking risks for learning (condition 1). From this base, we can nurture the capacity for learners to engage in Productive Puzzling. In Chapter 5, we will briefly describe the value of balancing challenges (condition 2) with attainable solutions (condition 3). We then explain how to teach learners about strategies (condition 4) and deliver feedback to engage them in self-reflection (condition 5).

Table 2.1 The Flexible Mindsets Spiral of Reflective Learning: Productive Puzzling

 **BE METACOGNITIVE**	Scan your lesson plans for opportunities to introduce puzzles. How will you help students understand the type of content that is best suited to using thinking and reasoning for Productive Puzzling versus content that is factual and can be learned with more traditional methods?
 **MODEL**	How will you model and encourage the questions that help us to use curiosity to explore new depths? "I wonder what would happen if . . ." "How can we use this new knowledge to imagine a different way of thinking about what we are learning?"
 **ASK QUESTIONS AND AFFORD TIME**	How will you schedule brief moments for unprogrammed time for students to puzzle, reflect or get bored?
 **USE SHARING AS A SPRINGBOARD**	How will you build in opportunities for students to share their stories about delving deeply into puzzles and how working hard leads to greater satisfaction? "I saw your group had a long discussion when you were struggling with building this robot. Share your challenges with the class and how you were able to work through them and find a solution together. How did you feel in the middle of the difficult work and how do you feel about having made the robot work? How did grappling with the challenges contribute to the process?"
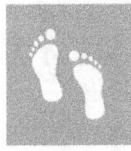 **THINK ON YOUR FEET**	How will you respond to unexpected moments by encouraging your students to turn curve balls into puzzles to be explored? "You probably weren't expecting this to happen. Why do you think it happened and how can you explore it further?"

References

Agarwal, P., & Bain, P. (2019). *Powerful teaching: Unleash the science of learning*. San Francisco, CA: Jossey-Bass.

Berlyne, D. (1960). *Conflict, arousal, and curiosity*. New York, NY: McGraw-Hill.

Duckworth, E. (2006). *"The having of wonderful ideas" and other essays on teaching and learning*. 3rd ed. New York, NY: Teachers College Press.

Elpidorou, A. (2014). The bright side of boredom. *Frontiers in Psychology* [online]. **5**, 1245. [Viewed 14 July 2019]. Available from: doi.10.3389/fpsyg.2014.01245

Gkiokas, D. (2018). How to utilize both brain's thinking modes: Focused vs diffuse [online]. *The Meta Learners*. [Viewed 12 March 2020]. Available from: https://www.themetalearners.com/how-to-utilize-both-brains-thinking-modes-focused-vs-diffuse/

Gruber, M., Gelman, B., & Ranganath, C. (2014). States of curiosity modulate hippocampus-dependent learning via the dopaminergic circuit. *Neuron*. **84**(2), 486–496.

Heick, T. (2019). From procedural knowledge to self knowledge: The 4 stages of curiosity [online]. *teachthought*. [Viewed 10 November 2019]. Available from: www.teachthought.com/learning/4-stages-of-curiosity/

Kashdan, T. (2004). Curiosity. In: C. Peterson & M. Seligman, eds. *Character strengths and virtues*. New York, NY: Oxford University Press. pp. 125–141.

Lazarus, R. (1991). *Emotion and adaptation*. New York, NY: Oxford University Press.

Meltzer, L. (2010). *Promoting executive function in the classroom*. New York, NY: Guilford Press.

Meltzer, L. (2013). Executive function processes: The foundation of academic and life success. *International Journal for Research in Learning Disabilities*. **1**(2), 31–63.

Medina, J. (2008). *Brain rules: 12 principles for surviving and thriving at work, home, and school*. Seattle, WA: Pear Press.

Oakley, B., & Sejnowski, T. (2018). *Learning how to learn: How to succeed in school without spending all your time studying*. New York, NY: Penguin Random House.

Peterson, S., & Posner, M. (2012). The attention system of the brain: 20 years after. *Annual review of neuroscience*. **35**, 73–89.

Sansone, C., & Thoman, D. (2005). Interest as the missing motivator in self-regulation. *European Psychologist*. **10**, 175–186.

Silvia, P. (2005). What is interesting? Exploring the appraisal structure of interest. *Emotion*. **5**, 89–102.

Silvia, P. (2006). *The psychology of interest*. New York, NY: Oxford University Press.

Silvia, P. (2008) Interest – The curious emotion. *Current Directions in Psychological Science.* **17**(1), 57–60.

Warshauer, H. (2015). Productive struggle in middle school mathematics classrooms. *Journal of Mathematics Teacher Education.* **18**(4), 375–400.

Willingham, D. (2009). *Why don't students like school? A cognitive scientist answers questions about how the mind works and what it means for your classroom.* New York, NY: Wiley.

Wilson, M. (2015). *The language of learning: Teaching students core thinking, listening and speaking skills.* Turner Falls, MA: Center for Responsive Schools, Inc.

Zomorodi, M. (2017). *Bored and brilliant: How spacing out can unlock your most productive and creative self.* New York, NY: St. Michael's Press.

SECTION II

Productive Puzzling conditions for transforming mindsets

CHAPTER 3

How do fixed mentalities close the window for learning?

Mindsets are more than a poster on the wall. Changing an institution's mindset culture can be incredibly challenging. There are many lifetimes of habits and fixed mentalities that hinder our efforts to make meaningful changes to the ways that we interact with our environment. Despite our efforts, the education system is remarkably stable and resistant to change, leaving some feeling the pace of innovation is 'one step forwards, two steps backwards'. Factors such as societal expectations and high stakes testing reinforce the slide towards the status quo. Within this context, fear of failure can send our brains automatically into survival mode, shutting down the pathways for learning.

The window of tolerance is a model founded by Dan Siegel, a Clinical Professor of Psychiatry at the UCLA School of Medicine. Using research about the nervous system, the window of tolerance offers a way of thinking about optimal arousal levels which allow us to function well and thrive. When we are within the window of tolerance, we are able to learn, play and relate well to ourselves and others. There is a natural ebb and flow to our emotions, including confusion and frustration, that we are generally able to navigate and stay within this window. However, when we feel strong emotions and our heightened states of alert remain constant over prolonged periods of time, we shift into hyperarousal states that are no longer optimal for learning (Siegal & Bryson 2012). In the Flexible Mindsets model, we reformulate this idea and use it to describe how hyperarousal of the nervous system can close the window for learning.

Think back to your years in school and a teacher who helped you want to learn more. What qualities did you like about this teacher? How did you feel in their company? What did they do or say to make you feel that way? Now think of a teacher you didn't trust. What did this teacher do or say? How motivated were you to learn from this teacher? What are some of the things you do or don't do as a professional that you can trace back to these experiences? How would you like your students to describe you?

Productive Puzzling conditions

> In this chapter, we lay out the natural implications of fixed mentalities that close the window on learning. Each section covers the driving forces that, if left unchecked, can lead to the deterioration of trust. As you will notice when you start to read Chapter 4, each driving force presented here is counteracted by the Flexible Mindsets framework:

Chapter 3	Chapter 4
Fear of failure	Trusting relationships
How do power and control close the window for learning?	How do co-creation and power sharing open the window for learning?
Values that close the window for learning	Values that open the window for learning
	Flexible Mindsets Language

Fear of failure

Most educational settings are steeped in fixed mentalities about intelligence, including myths about marginalised students, especially those who learn differently. For a student who struggles, expectations are low: system-level messages tell both teachers and students that there are predetermined limits on how much the student can learn. Conversely, for students who perform well in classrooms, fixed mentality systems send the message that 'smart' students must always answer swiftly and accurately; and that mistakes are a sign of failure and low intelligence. These expectations leave the student trapped in the need to appear smart and not make mistakes.

Researchers have been studying fear of failure for decades. The often quoted classic *Pygmalion in the Classroom* illustrates the story of teacher influences on the self-fulfilling prophecies of students. Researchers conducted a study with first through sixth grade students in which they manipulated the expectations of teachers (Rosenthal & Jacobsen 1968). The researchers informed the teachers that the children had been assessed on a measure of ability that was, in fact, fictional. Instead of using actual scores to identify children who were 'gifted', the authors randomly selected students and informed the teachers that these students were 'growth spurters' and expected to make dramatic gains over the course of the school year. Teacher expectations strongly predicted student performance at the end of the school year. In fact, they were more predictive than the students' actual IQ scores as assessed at the beginning of the year.

This study elucidated the process that many children experience as they proceed through the educational system: a cycle where failure or disruptive behaviour interacts with the beliefs and negative messages from others, reinforcing negative self-perceptions and increasing the likelihood of failure and more disruptive behaviour. These self-fulfilling prophecies, once established, can be enduring.

Historically, experts in the fields of social psychology and learning have studied the patterns of how we explain the causality of our successes, failures and the events in our lives by referring to external and internal factors. This is referred to as attribution theory (Heider 1957; Weiner 1972). Individuals with negative attribution styles tend to overlook their successes, expect failure and therefore give up more quickly. This can be especially true for nonprivileged students, who are typically punished at a higher rate than their peers for the same infractions. This cycle reinforces the self-fulfilling prophecy of low persistence and repeated failure. Other researchers have translated attribution theory and applied it directly to the notions of learned helplessness and learned optimism (Seligman 2006; Dweck 1975; Dweck & Goetz 1978). We can recognise learned helplessness when students attribute failure to something that is an inherent trait such as "I'm stupid". At the same time, they discount successes on a test or assignment with thoughts like: "That was so easy – everyone did well" or "Today must be my lucky day!" or "The teacher felt sorry for me and gave me extra points." These attributions for success and failure have considerable consequences in terms of causal beliefs and their emotional and motivational significance. In other words, encouragement and a few successes is not enough to turn around the mindset of a student with learned helplessness. When children feel this discouraged, the window can close on their chances of becoming resilient and flexible.

On the flip side of this coin, people with fixed mentalities who view themselves as smart will tend to disregard failures and will use successes to reinforce their positive self-perceptions (Blackwell, Trzesniewski & Dweck 2007; Boaler 2010). However, they may become primarily invested in making no mistakes in order to protect their self-image. Children who are repeatedly told they are smart grow up feeling they have to be perfect: get the highest test scores, excel in more than one domain and get into the best universities. Their families exert a great deal of effort towards these ends: completing assignments to improve their children's grades, reviewing and drilling in preparation for tests, arguing with teachers who provide constructive feedback and avoiding 'failure' at all costs. Speed of completing assignments is seen as a sign of high intelligence, irrespective of the depths to which concepts have been understood and applied. Deeper thinkers who carefully and extensively explore an idea are often called 'slow processors' and their capabilities are dismissed. Children who think outside of the box and make novel connections are seen as having difficulty understanding assignments and as unable to meet the requirements for closed-ended tasks.

So, whether you are at the top, middle or bottom of the class, you may dread failure and avoid taking risks as a part of learning.

The historical work on learned helplessness has, to an extent, helped us to understand the psychological processes that account for fear of failure and reluctance to take learning-related risks. Solutions to these challenges, however, are tougher to find. For decades, educators and other professionals have endeavoured to counteract the destructive effects of school failure on the outlook and engagement of students. We have tried encouragement, skills training, structured successes, peer mentoring and differentiated instruction, with limited and inconsistent results.

You may remember Jelani's experiences from Chapter 1. His journey continues here:

> By the time the middle of the school year rolled around, Jelani was showing up at school tired and appeared uninterested in learning. School was no longer a place where he felt emotionally safe and he had come to expect negative feedback from teachers. He didn't always remember to do his homework or hand it in and he did the bare minimum on projects, just enough to hand something in. When he received feedback about what he could do to plan and organise his ideas, he became preoccupied with all the things that prevented him from planning and organising (such as a lack of time), rather than staying open to trying something new. His teachers began to see him as rigid because he did not follow their advice. But, for Jelani, planning ahead and studying for tests seemed like a waste of time, since he was going to fail anyway. He would just 'wing it' and hope for the best. Jelani's grades started reflecting his lack of preparation and teacher comments on his report card suggested he was capable but needed to work harder if he was going to pass. His window was barely open at this point . . .
>
> By the start of the final term of the school year, the pressure from his parents and teachers had only grown and Jelani was left feeling like it was all on him to turn things around. Despite wanting to make his parents proud of him and to hear positive feedback from his teachers, Jelani had shut down to the extent that he couldn't even begin. It was easier to give up and just prove to everyone that he wasn't able to do it than to try to figure out what to change. His window was closed.

It is Jelani's memories of feeling disappointed, frustrated and humiliated that constitute his fear. According to Ned Hallowell, "the greatest learning disorder of all is fear" (Hallowell n.d.; 2012). Public humiliation is the most salient memory of danger that many children experience. Humiliation and shaming take on a variety of different forms that can be subtle and unintentional and leave a student feeling like they did something wrong or that they are not good enough.

This evokes a flood of negative feelings originating in the amygdala, the area of the brain that detects threats. It triggers the fight, flight or freeze response that hijacks the prefrontal cortex and leaves us unable to think clearly. In short, the more the amygdala is constantly detecting threats, the less we are able to think (Center on the Developing Child at Harvard University 2021). For students like Jelani, this toxic stress closes the window for learning (see Figure 3.1).

As educators, we often inadvertently exacerbate the impact of toxic stress and Adverse Childhood Experiences (ACEs) by using coded language related to seeing children as 'at-risk'. If we couch a child's trauma in risk factors, it is easy to fall into the trap of blaming the child, that child's family or the neighbourhood. This may absolve us from feeling that we have to address the failings of an oppressive

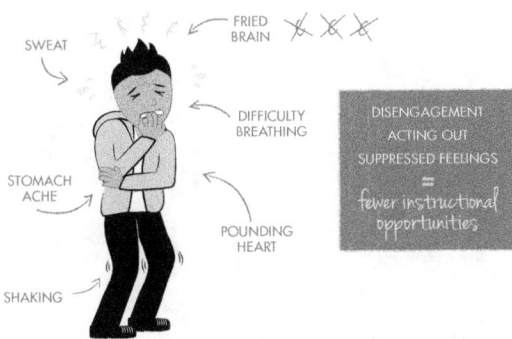

Figure 3.1 Closing the window for learning

educational system but can ultimately close a child's window for learning today and tomorrow. ACEs are the unrelenting stress caused by poverty, neglect, abuse, household violence, caregiver mental illness, racism, community violence that can weaken the architecture of the developing brain (Center on the Developing Child at Harvard University 2018).

Children can be misunderstood as their parents and teachers search for reasons to explain why an otherwise intelligent child is not producing 'results' consistent with his or her 'abilities'. We may erroneously conclude that a child doesn't try hard, is lazy or is unmotivated. The truth is that children like Jelani are very motivated to 'hold it together'; they spend the whole school day expending their mental energy in survival mode.

More recent research has helped us better understand what happens in the brain when students are repeatedly exposed to stress. Neuroimaging studies of the limbic system along with measurement of the chemicals released in the brain during the learning process reveal that a student's level of comfort significantly impacts how information is transmitted and stored in the brain (Thanos et al. 1999). If you don't have any stress, then there will be no physiological reaction, leaving low energy levels, and your brain is less activated. To create and strengthen neural pathways, we do need some stress. A low level of stress is a good thing because it helps us to recruit the resources needed to reach a goal (Jain 2015). It activates the brain and gears us up to cope with challenging situations. Stress can be referred to as 'good stress' when the level of challenge is within our reach. As illustrated in Figure 3.2, this is what is referred to as the 'stress sweet spot': not too much and not too little (Friedman 2018).

With just the right amount of stress, our bodies will secrete the hormones adrenaline and cortisol to help prepare our bodies to respond quickly to a threat. The burst of cortisol triggers our bodies to release glucose for energy and adrenaline to increase our attention. A small amount of cortisol also enhances the growth

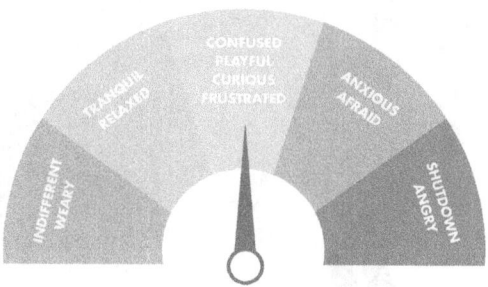

Figure 3.2 The 'sweet spot' for learning

of neurons in the hippocampus, the part of the brain that plays an important role in learning and memory (McEwen 2017).

Too much stress, or chronic stress, has the opposite effect (Center on the Developing Child at Harvard University 2018; 2021). When our bodies pump out excessive amounts of adrenaline and cortisol, and if this persists over time, our brains shut down. When the brain is flooded with adrenaline and cortisol, the neural pathways related to the prefrontal cortex are cut off. And what part of the brain is needed for us to think critically, solve problems and be creative? The prefrontal cortex. We often forget that chronic stress also tends to impact a person's quality of sleep and if you are not sleeping deeply, your brain's ability to perform neurogenesis (generating new neurons) will be impaired (McEwen 2017).

Oftentimes, we may not fully understand the challenges of intergenerational trauma where the damage experienced by previous generations is carried over and can be further compounded by punitive systems, increasing a child's vulnerability. For students to better understand how anxiety is affecting their lives, the iceberg model can be a helpful tool. They are often unaware, themselves, that their surface behaviours are rooted in underlying stress and anxiety. We may hear a child's personal story and view it as merely an explanation, rather than finding ways to meet our students where they are.

How do power and control close the window for learning?

Imagine that you are in a restaurant, having dinner with some friends. The bread rolls arrive and everyone takes a roll. A short while later, being still hungry, you reach towards the breadbasket again. One of your friends, who wants to support you, says "Really! I thought you were trying to *lose* weight!" How does that make you feel? It depends. It depends on how much effort you have put into your weight loss goal, your friend's tone of voice and body language, the reactions of your other friends and the reactions of the other people in the restaurant. If these things work against you, they can make you feel embarrassed and helpless. What if, instead of friends, it was a work outing and the person who questioned your commitment to your goal was your boss? How would that change the way you felt? Ultimately, it is the *power differential* that determines how vulnerable you are.

Now think about the students you are currently working with. Do they all react similarly when you correct them in class? Which students may feel more vulnerable? What factors affect how vulnerable they feel?

We all need a sense of agency over our own lives. We feel safe when we can predict what may happen, change the things we can, and accept and cope with ongoing and new challenges. Our comfort zones, no matter how self-limiting, feel safer than the unknown. Without a sense of competence we are unable to work actively towards goals and aspirations. Students have no choice but to cede control to the adults in their lives. They are forced to become vulnerable and hope that we will uphold their trust. Sadly, in many settings, the goals of the system are pursued at the expense of children's needs.

When control is the goal, rather than learning, classroom management consists of hierarchical, punitive measures, leaving student engagement out of the equation. If we recognise that systems of shaming and punishment were the early weapons for colonialism and slavery, we can take the first step towards becoming a co-learner, coach or a facilitator.

Sometimes, when students aren't doing what we have asked, it is because they don't understand the instructions, or the task is too complex and they don't have the prerequisite skills to be able to tackle the task. Sometimes, the biggest challenges to engagement can be things that have happened outside of school and are weighing heavily on a child's mind and heart.

As adults, we often misinterpret a child's actions when they are not working towards a goal that we have set. Children's personal goals often differ from what we think they should be working on. The boy who is looking out the window, instead of working on the task we have set, may have a goal of avoiding a difficult task or perhaps of learning more about the construction site next door. Although these are purposeful goals, they are not always working towards what we believe is in the child's best interests. Adults need to take the lead in working with learners to identify the meaning and value of goals that will serve them in the long run. Underlying the behaviours we see on the surface – avoidance, lack of focus and defiance – are layers of emotions and experiences that students bury within themselves: embarrassment, insecurity, negativity and rejection. As with the iceberg model, students are often penalised for the surface behaviours without consideration of the underlying unmet needs. We may have to dig a little deeper to figure out why a student is overwhelmed or appears as if they don't want to do what is being asked of them, to uncover missing skills or social and emotional challenges (Greene 2014).

Emotions matter when it comes to learning. Our ability to pay attention is directly related to how we feel. If a student is feeling nervous, bullied or neglected at home, how can we expect them to be able to focus their attention on learning about gravity? Marc Brackett is the Founding Director of the Yale Center for Emotional Intelligence. In his book *Permission to Feel* (2019), he describes his troubled childhood and the powerful healing he experienced when an adult he trusted acknowledged his feelings and helped him to learn emotion skills. All any of us want is to feel safe and loved.

Values that close the window for learning

John Holt (Holt & Fromme 1964, p. 44) likens fear of failure to "Walking a tightrope." He describes his students as being too afraid to step out onto the tightrope of trying. Our students often feel safer with the knowledge that they have failed, rather than teetering along wondering when they will fall. They often appear relieved to have adults confirm that they have gotten something wrong. As the old saying goes "You can't fall out of bed if you sleep on the floor". Today's systems appear structured to ensure that many of our students are sleeping on the floor.

Fixed mentalities permeate most educational institutions and society as a whole. They tell us that there are smart people and then there are people who aren't so smart (Dweck 2008; 2017). They *assume that abilities are fixed and that we cannot get smarter*. There is an inherent set of values that define fixed mentalities and close the window for learning.

Does working hard mean I'm stupid?

People often assume that if someone has to work hard, they are not smart. This sentiment is prevalent and can be found in overt and subtle messages we hear every day, both in school and in the broader community. Cartoonist Bill Watterson captures this message adeptly in one of his Calvin and Hobbes comic strips (2015). Calvin is baffled by the amount of work that Susie does. She explains that, because she didn't fully understand a chapter, she reviewed her notes from the previous chapter and is rereading the current chapter. Calvin says, "You do all that *work*!" and concludes "Huh! I used to think you were smart." This false notion that intelligence and effort are inversely related works counterproductively when engaged in reasoning, problem-solving and creative endeavours. It also contradicts the research in cognitive science that suggests that slowing down and exerting mental effort will make "learning stronger, more precise and more enduring" (Brown, Roediger & McDaniel 2014, p. 68). Learning how to appreciate and get comfortable with feeling frustrated and confused is essential to learning because, when we feel these things, our brains are rewiring themselves.

Learning and adapting involves breaking old neural pathways and forming new, oftentimes more complex neural pathways. When we dig into learning something new, we may hit a threshold that feels so uncomfortable that we give up. We need to be able to acknowledge our frustration and reframe it by reminding ourselves that this is a sign our brain is learning, growing and adapting. As we push through our feelings of frustration, new neural pathways are formed and eventually they become strong and we feel confident in this new area of learning. Rather than seeing frustration and confusion as indicators of stupidity, they are an indication that we are on the pathway toward learning and our brains are 'levelling up' (Craig et al. 2004). We know from history, and our own life experiences, that many inventions and innovations have resulted from working intensively for extended periods of time, experiencing frustration and confusion and reframing mistakes as learning opportunities.

Does asking questions mean I'm stupid?

Children and adults often feel afraid to ask questions because they think it will make them look stupid. Many students report that they only feel comfortable speaking and asking questions in class when they know that they have the 'correct' answer, their views are consistent with their peers and they are certain they won't disappoint their teachers. Those who feel safe asking questions to which they don't know the answer usually have more positive self-perceptions, take on more difficult challenges, persevere when struggling and view mistakes as opportunities to learn.

> "I don't want to seem stupid asking questions in front of the other students if they might already know the answer."

> "I feel some teachers don't want to know if I'm struggling, so what's the point of bothering them if it just makes them more irritated with me."

> "I just wish the teacher would notice when I get things right instead of just pointing out what I do wrong."

If the leaders I see don't look like me, are people who look like me stupid?

In 2016, a survey by the US Department of Education found that 82% of public school teachers identified as white. In the United States, black males make up only 2% of the teaching workforce. In 2018 The College Board narrowed the scope of its World History Advanced Placement Exam to range from c. 1450 to the present (Wong 2018). The new test removes over 9,000 years of history from the birth of Confucianism to the expansion of the West African Kingdoms. Underrepresentation of Black, Indigenous and People of Colour is just one of the cogs in a system built to perpetuate racism and other forms of social injustice. Targeted strategies to increase representation in the education field and curriculum are a start, but not enough. Students also need to see people that look like them who are highlighting a counternarrative to the dominant white culture.

If I take a long time to answer questions and complete my work, am I stupid?

The need for speed is disproportionately valued in traditional educational settings. When the teacher asks a question, who raises their hands the fastest? On quizzes and tests, who finishes first? How much are students penalised for handing in assignments after the due date? Why aren't all students given the time they need to complete high stakes tests? If we look behind the curtain, we have to admit that a part of us believes that speed is a sign of intelligence. Where does this leave the students who are predisposed to think critically, solve messy problems and be creative?

If my test scores are low, am I stupid?

Standardisation in curricula and testing is an archaic and oppressive practice that devalues other ways of knowing. Benchmark testing discriminates in favour of white, privileged children whose learning profiles favour oral and written language. The overemphasis on the 3R's comes at the cost of the 3C's and eliminates a broader set of educational outcomes that offer full and purposeful ways of being. Children with strengths such as relationship building, Creativity and empathy end up feeling inadequate and somehow lesser.

Given these values that permeate our schools, self-directed learning can only be achieved through meaningful transformation. By explicitly teaching learners about beliefs related to intelligence and how we have the power to change our own mindsets, we can begin to lessen feelings of being overwhelmed. It is essential that we make I CAN messages prevalent in the learning environment and teach learners how to envision positive images of themselves. As we learn about the brain, how it develops and what intelligence really is, we realise that we have the power to influence how our brain develops and that we can get smarter. Through a growing awareness of our thoughts and feelings, we can learn strategies to shift from emotional responses attributed to the amygdala to our 'thinking' brain in the prefrontal cortex. This allows us to be in control of the process, take ownership of learning, and journey further along the course of self-direction. For ideas to get started, refer to Table 3.1.

Ultimately, in Flexible Mindsets classrooms, trusting relationships will be prioritised and students will hear through our words and actions that we believe all students are capable and can learn. Our relentless belief is that "Every child deserves a champion: an adult who will never give up on them, who understands the power of connection and insists they become the best they can possibly be" (Pierson 2013).

Table 3.1 The Flexible Mindsets Spiral of Reflective Learning: closing the window for learning

 **BE METACOGNITIVE**	How will you help your students understand the effects of stress on the brain? How can you introduce the idea and language of the 'strained' brain and the 'thinking' brain? Which interactive learning tools will you use (diagrams, skits, models, etc.)?
 **MODEL**	What language will you use to communicate your belief that students are doing the best they can with the skills they have? How will you convey that you are in this with them as a problem-solver, rather than a disciplinarian? "Although you can't write the story on your own yet, there are some pieces we can work on first to build this skill."
 **ASK QUESTIONS AND AFFORD TIME**	What new questions will you use with students to reduce their fear of failure? "I know you are discouraged and don't feel like studying for tomorrow's test. What is one question you have that you can explore and quiz yourself on tonight?" "I understand that it can be scary to participate in class discussions. What do you wonder about when you think of ____? Are you willing to ask that question when we talk about this tomorrow?"
 **USE SHARING AS A SPRINGBOARD**	How will you co-create ground rules and guide discussions to communicate that all ideas are valued and that humiliation is not welcome? "Let's come up with some rules for our group discussions that will ensure that everyone feels safe to share ideas and that everyone's voice is heard."
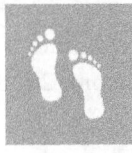 **THINK ON YOUR FEET**	What strategies and responses can you pull out of your toolkit when frustration, anxiety and stress become evident? "It sounds like you are feeling anxious about this task. Let's break it down into smaller chunks and make a plan together for how you can complete one chunk at a time."

References

Blackwell, L., Trzesniewski, K., & Dweck, C. (2007). Implicit theories of intelligence predict achievement across an adolescent transition: A longitudinal study and an intervention. *Child Development.* **78**(1), 246–263.

Boaler, J. (2010). *The elephant in the classroom: Helping children learn and love maths.* London, UK: Souvenir Press.

Brackett, M. (2019). *Permission to feel: Unlocking the power of emotions to help our kids, ourselves, and our society thrive.* New York, NY: Celadon Books.

Brown, P., Roediger, H., & McDaniel, M. (2014). *Make it stick: The science of successful learning.* Cambridge, MA: The Belknap Press of Harvard University Press.

Center on the Developing Child at Harvard University. (2018). ACE's and toxic stress: Frequently asked questions [infographic]. *The President and Fellows of Harvard College.* [Viewed 9 September 2019]. Available from: https://developingchild.harvard.edu/resources/aces-and-toxic-stress-frequently-asked-questions/

Center on the Developing Child at Harvard University. (2021). Toxic stress [online]. *The President and Fellows of Harvard College.* [Viewed 9 September 2019]. Available from: https://developingchild.harvard.edu/science/key-concepts/toxic-stress/

Craig, S., Graesser, A., Sullins, J., & Gholson, B. (2004). Affect and learning: An exploratory look into the role of affect in learning with AutoTutor. *Journal of Educational Media* [online]. **29**(3), 241–250. [Viewed 4 October 2020]. Available from: doi: 10.1080/1358165042000283101

Dr. Hallowell: Living a better life. (2012). Mrs Eldredge, my first grade teacher [online]. *YouTube.* [Viewed 13 July 2019]. Available from: www.youtube.com/watch?v=7Z6bD4Fz6rY

Dweck, C. (1975). The role of expectations and attributions in the alleviation of learned helplessness. *Journal of Personality and Social Psychology.* **31**(4), 674–685.

Dweck, C. (2008). *Mindset: The new psychology of success.* New York, NY: Ballantine.

Dweck, C. (2017). *Mindset: Changing the way you think to fulfil your potential.* New York, NY: Robinson.

Dweck, C., & Goetz, T. (1978). Attributions and learned helplessness. In: J. Harvey, W. Ickes, & R. Kidds, eds. *New directions in attribution research.* New York, NY: Wiley. pp. 158–175.

Friedman, R. A. (2018). The stress sweet spot. *The New York Times* [online]. 1 June 2018. [Viewed 4 October 2019]. Available from: www.nytimes.com/2018/06/01/opinion/stress-students-kids-brains-sleep.html

Greene, R. (2014). *Lost at school: Why our kids with behavioral challenges are falling through the cracks and how we can help them.* New York, NY: Scribner.

Hallowell, N. (n.d.). ADHD – Changing the shame and fear [online]. *Dr Hallowell.* [Viewed 2 May 2019]. Available from: www.drhallowell.com/the-shame-and-fear-of-adhd/

Heider, F. (1957). *The psychology of interpersonal relations.* New York, NY: Wiley.

Holt, J. & Fromme, A. (1964). *How children fail.* New York, NY: Pitman.

Jain, R. (2015). Can stress help students? [online]. *edutopia.* 9 February 2015. [Viewed 17 July 2019]. Available from: www.edutopia.org/blog/can-stress-help-students-renee-jain

McEwen, B. (2017). Neurobiological and systemic effects of chronic stress. *Chronic Stress* [online]. **1**, 1–11. [Viewed 14 July 2019]. Available from: doi:10.1177/2470547017692328

Pierson, R. (2013). Every kid needs a champion [online]. *TED Talks Education.* [Viewed 2 May 2020]. Available from: www.ted.com/talks/rita_pierson_every_kid_needs_a_champion?language=en.

Rosenthal, R., & Jacobsen, L. (1968). *Pygmalion in the classroom: Teacher expectation and pupils' intellectual development.* New York, NY: Holt, Rinehart and Winston.

Seligman, M. (2006). *Learned optimism: How to change your mind and your life.* New York, NY: Vintage.

Siegal, D., & Bryson, T. (2012). *The whole-brain child: 12 revolutionary strategies to nurture your child's developing mind.* New York, NY: Random House Inc.

Thanos, P., Katana, J., Ashby, C., Michaelides, M., Gardner, E., Heidbreder, C., et al. (1999). The selective dopamine D3 receptor antagonist SB-277011-A attenuates ethanol consumption in ethanol preferring (P) and nonpreferring (NP) rats. *Pharmacology, Biochemistry, and Behavior.* **81**(1), 190–197.

US Department of Education, Office of Planning, Evaluation and Policy Development, Policy and Program Studies Service. (2016). *The state of racial diversity in the educator workforce.* Washington, DC: United States Department of Education.

Watterson, B. (2005). *The complete Calvin and Hobbes.* Kansas City, MO: Andrew McMeel Publishing.

Weiner, B. (1972). Attribution theory, achievement motivation, and the educational process. *Review of Educational Research.* **42**(2), 203–215.

Wong, A. (2018). The Controversy over just how much history AP world history should cover. *The Atlantic* [online]. 13 June 2018. [Viewed 14 March 2019]. Available from: www.theatlantic.com/education/archive/2018/06/ap-world-history-controversy/562778/

CHAPTER

Building trusting relationships to open the window for learning (condition 1)

Hitting the kill switch

Kathy Hannun was previously a Product Manager on the Rapid Evaluation team at X (formerly called Google[x]). As a Rapid Evaluator, her role was to find new opportunities for X and look for reasons to pull the plug on a project even if it was her own. To make this decision, she asked herself "What is the thing that will bring this project down?" One of Kathy's project ideas was to turn seawater into fuel called 'Fog Horn'. She established a kill signal to keep herself and her team honest: for this project to be successful, they could not go over a cost of $5.00 a gallon for the fuel. Just thinking about the kill signal really helped her team think through the complexity of the problem they were trying to solve. They got to work on the project and tackled many obstacles until they discovered an issue with pumping the seawater – the pumping energy required to pump the seawater to extract CO_2 had an astronomically high cost. Kathy decided to write an email acknowledging the vision, all the amazing things they had accomplished and the obstacles they had overcome, but also highlighting the challenges. Having weighed all the data they currently had, she recommended that Fog Horn be shut down. The project had failed. Although Kathy wasn't happy the project failed, she was able to recognise that she did a good job of being a Rapid Evaluator. You'll find out later on in this chapter how Kathy and the culture at X made it possible to value failure.

(Grant 2021)

This chapter challenges us to build trusting relationships that help students feel comfortable to ask questions, make mistakes and take risks for learning. In Chapter 3, we laid out the natural implications of fixed mentalities that close the window on learning. Now, in Chapters 4 and 5, we return to the necessary conditions for Productive Puzzling that we introduced in Chapter 2. Each section corresponds a driving force raised in Chapter 3 as follows:

Chapter 3	Chapter 4
Fear of failure	Trusting relationships
How do power and control close the window for learning?	How do co-creation and power sharing open the window for learning?
Values that close the window for learning	Values that open the window for learning
	Flexible Mindsets Language

Trusting relationships

As Dr Robert Brooks notes, it is difficult to adopt a growth mindset without fostering a sense of belonging, caring and connectedness with all of our students (Brooks 2015; n.d.). As the first condition necessary for Productive Puzzling, trusting relationships form the cornerstone of Flexible Mindsets (see Figure 4.1).

The ability to build trust in the classroom rests on relationships that communicate a genuine belief that students are inherently well intentioned, and they do well if they can (Greene 2014). If we can shift our thinking from the student who doesn't want to do it to the student who can't do it *yet*, our role is transformed from disciplinarian to coach or facilitator. By establishing trust in the space that surrounds you, you help learners to feel secure enough to explore, take learning-related risks and bring all of themselves to learning. As more and more zones of trust are incorporated within a school, a Flexible Mindsets ethos replaces the traditional, fixed mentalities culture.

Dr Ned Hallowell, renowned child psychiatrist, often tells the story of his first grade teacher, Ms Eldridge. When he entered school, young Ned had significant challenges with learning to read. Instead of making him afraid of being ridiculed, the teacher put her arm around him when it was his turn to read aloud. Today, Dr Hallowell attributes much of his confidence to Mrs Eldridge's intervention and how it made him feel safe (Dr Hallowell 2012).

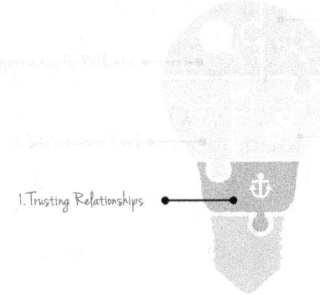

Figure 4.1 Trusting relationships: condition 1 for Productive Puzzling

This evidence reminds us that it is part of our role to make school safe for children to be who they are. The antidote to fear is courage. Courage arises from people like Ned Hallowell's teacher, Ms Eldridge. If you have someone in your life who believes in you, they become the safety net that allows you to take risks (Brooks 2018). When someone has faith that you are capable, they are taking leadership in modelling trust. Leadership does not come from power and authority. Leaders are those who trust first. It is our responsibility to ensure that learners don't have to dig deep to find courage (Sinek 2009). They need us to trust first, believe in them and counteract their fears. When students feel safe and valued for who they are, they can build the trust needed to take risks, challenge themselves and persevere.

Trust is even more important for children like Jelani who we introduced in Chapter 1. These students often experience toxic stress that closes the window for learning. In these cases, the remedy lies in fostering those trusting relationships that create spaces where learners are comfortable asking questions, making mistakes and taking risks for learning.

> When Jelani first started coming to coaching sessions, he found it hard to hear any feedback about his work. When asked how it made him feel to hear constructive comments about how he could improve his work, he said it made him feel bad about himself because he wanted to see himself as smart. If there was something he could have done differently, it must mean that he isn't smart enough. Through exploring more about how the brain learns, open discussions about his unique strengths and challenges, and ongoing feedback, his negative self-perceptions started to shift towards being more realistic.

Without this trusting relationship with his executive function coach, Jelani may never have reengaged with learning. Jelani needed to get the message that he is capable and that his brain can continue to learn. To help students do this, we need to change our own mindsets and relearn what we mean by intelligence.

Recent work in the field of growth mindsets has debunked many of the traditional ways that we view intelligence (Dweck 2008). There are numerous studies that support the notion that neuroplasticity of the brain extends beyond childhood. For example, structural MRIs were used to compare the posterior hippocampi of licensed London taxi cab drivers to those of a control group who did not drive taxis. The volume of the posterior hippocampus correlated positively with the amount of time spent driving a taxi. Results supported the authors' theory that the posterior hippocampus stores spatial representations and that it can be larger in people with a high dependence on navigational skills (Maguire et al. 2000).

It is from studies like this that we can begin to rethink our own values and open the window for learning.

How do co-creation and power sharing open the window for learning?

In Chapter 3, we noted how feelings of helplessness contribute to fixed mentalities. One strategy for counteracting these mindsets is to use *co-creation, the receptive and intentional use of student input to inform content delivery, instructional methods and the learning environment.* Involving students in co-creation affords learners some choice, thereby allowing them to feel a sense of agency. Co-creation is a simple way to help students to develop metacognitive awareness about how they learn and to empower them by including them in decisions about the setting, content and ways to show what they know. Metacognitive Insights about ourselves and environmental factors can make the difference between reaching our goals, or not. An additional benefit of co-creation is that you don't have to rely on knowing all the right answers to be respected. As learning becomes increasingly shared, you make deeper connections with your students, model metacognitive processes and empower them to target their own goals.

The physical setup of traditional teacher-centred classrooms is symbolic of our oppressive history. Changing learning spaces is a powerful tool for dismantling privileged structures and sharing power. In asking for student input regarding the environment, we must bear in mind that changing the physical environment goes hand in hand with content delivery. By giving them choice, we begin to empower students to become more self-directed. The simple act of asking them and incorporating their ideas gives them the message that their voices are heard and valued. Some questions you can use to engage your students in the decision-making process may include: *How much of the factual material will be delivered outside of class time through videos and notetaking? How much time will be dedicated to deeper exploration during a lesson or the school day? How can we rearrange our space to maximise your learning? For virtual learning, how will you use adult supervised breakout rooms and co-hosting?*

Co-creation begins when you ask your students about their interests and the ways that they like to explore and learn. As you continuously engage in this exchange, everyone becomes a more flexible thinker. Co-creation empowers students to take control over their own learning, explore ideas in greater depth and to move towards becoming self-directed.

Power sharing in the classroom places more ownership on students for their learning and shifts the role of the teacher from one of authority to one of co-learner. Students are no longer viewed as receptors of learning. When teachers spend less time trying to make lessons fun, they can shift to teaching brain-based strategies that students can use to make their own learning more engaging. They can also involve students in co-creation of content and spend more class time as a coach. In seeing ourselves as coaches, it is helpful to use analogies such as that used by Zaretta Hammond (2015) who compares the role of the teacher to a personal fitness trainer. In other words, your personal trainer does not do the push ups for you, but teaches you what a push up is and why it is important and then coaches you as you learn to do push ups on your own. Through this process, we put students in charge of their learning and give them tools they can apply throughout life. Sharing power improves motivation and engagement, gradually accelerating students along the track of self-directed learning.

Sharing power in classrooms draws on many of the concepts of Bill Miller and Stephen Rollnick's *Motivational Interviewing* that lay the groundwork for creating change (2013). It is based on the guiding principles of honouring a person's autonomy, kindling the inherent desire to change and being collaborative, not confrontational. Motivational interviewing techniques – balancing good listening with being directive, empowering people to change by drawing out their own meaning and cultivating a respectful and curious way of being to honour a person's autonomy – are all useful techniques when looking for strategies to create power sharing in our classrooms (Miller & Rollnick 2013).

We are all familiar with what teacher-centred classrooms look like and even child-centred classrooms. But what does a shared power, partner-centred classroom look like? In a *partner-centred classroom, teachers and students share the power and the workload, thereby creating a dynamic characterised by reciprocal flow, lively exchanges and intrinsically driven motion.*

Teachers are often aware that they wield a great deal of power over their students and that this diminishes independent learning. Yet educators are left feeling unsure of how to empower students without losing control of the learning process (see Figure 4.2). It's scary to equalise your relationship with students. If we suddenly woke up today and gave all the power over to our students, a multitude of disasters might occur. You may question: "How will students know who is in charge in the classroom? How productive will students be if I'm not directing them? How will we meet our learning outcomes? How will I know that students are striking the right balance between looking up facts and thinking for themselves?" What

Figure 4.2 Uncertainties about power sharing in the classroom

concerns come to your mind when you think about sharing more power with your students?

In order to avoid chaos, sharing power must be undertaken gradually and intentionally as we reframe the environment to reflect values that open the window for learning.

Values that open the window for learning

Intelligence is not predetermined

Every brain learns and develops differently, and we all have brains capable of getting smarter. Growth mindsets encourage us to focus feedback on things that the learner can have some control over such as effort, persistence and grit (Dweck 2008; Duckworth et al. 2007). However, approaches that focus solely on effort often inadvertently place blame on the student and send the message that they need to just try harder even when toxic stress is restricting neural pathways. This can further traumatise learners, especially those who have been marginalised. It makes no sense to expect children to not see themselves as victims when we have neither provided safety for them to take risks, nor given them the tools to learn HOW to learn. External markers such as grades give some indication of what's working and not working for a student; however, they are not an indication of how smart or capable he or she is. It's important for students to refocus their mental energy on those attributes they can influence by uncovering what they don't know, persevering and learning new strategies. These are the true markers of intelligence.

What we don't know

According to Eleanor Duckworth, "knowing the right answer requires no decision, carries no risks and makes no demands" (2006, p. 1). The essence of learning lies in knowing what we don't know and then digging in by thinking through, juggling, sorting, figuring out and grappling. The act of knowing what you don't know is the impetus for self-directed learning. If you already know everything about a topic you're not learning.

Traditional views describe intelligence as the ability to think and learn. Yet this is not what we value and test for in schools. The higher rewards in schools often favour speed and accuracy. If we were to redirect this level of enthusiasm to focus on the exploration of what we don't know, then curiosity and puzzling would have the greater value. Adam Grant takes it one step further by arguing that "in a turbulent world there's another set of cognitive skills that might matter more: the ability to *rethink* and *unlearn*" (2021, p. 2).

Mistakes and failures

We are born to explore. During the first three years, one of our most powerful teachers is our own mistakes. *Yuck! That tastes terrible, I'm not putting that in my mouth again. Ouch! That hurt – I'm not doing that again.*

Everyone makes mistakes. Despite the best of intentions, our choices, actions and inaction can result in unforeseen consequences or unwanted results. Mistakes usually cause some degree of distress or discomfort. With this frame of mind, it is understandable that so many of us avoid situations where we might make mistakes.

Nonetheless, we now know that learners who see errors as genuine growth opportunities do not see mistakes as a threat to their self-concept. They actively seek challenging problems that will trigger an error message. When we immerse ourselves in activities that are perplexing, we may reduce the frequency of quick wins, but sustained growth and innovation thrive (Tulis, Steuer & Dresel 2016).

Recent research has shed light on the neural underpinnings of the associations between mindsets and responses to errors. Whenever synapses fire, we are learning, even if it is not conscious. For example, researchers at Michigan State University measured electrical brain signals (firing synapses) that are related to internal monitoring of performance. The first type of signals are ERNs (error related negativity) and occur in the part of the brain used for self-monitoring. The second set of signals originate in the part of the brain used to focus attention to possible mistakes Pe's (error response positivity). Whether or not students had a fixed or growth mindset, increased electrical activity was noted in response to mistakes (Moser et al. 2011). This is consistent with the views of experts like Jo Boaler who says,

> When teachers ask me how this can be possible, I tell them that the best thinking we have on this now is that the brain sparks and grows when we make a mistake, even if we are not aware of it, because it is a time of struggle; the brain is challenged and the challenge results in growth.
>
> (Boaler 2010, p. 11)

Learning from mistakes is further enhanced in individuals with growth mindsets. For example, in the study described, growth mindsets were associated with higher electrical activity in the part of the brain that allocates attention to mistakes. Furthermore, this enhanced error positivity was associated with more correct responses following errors (Moser et al. 2011). In other words, all brains grow from making mistakes. In addition, learners with growth mindsets are more likely to monitor their work for errors, be on the alert for mistakes they have previously made, and ultimately make fewer repetitive errors. Furthermore, by directly teaching strategies for managing hyperarousal in the brain, we can help learners spend more time in the window of tolerance (Seigal & Bryson 2012).

To build trusting relationships, we must transform the dominant mindset into one that acknowledges mistakes as holding greater value for learning than seamlessly arriving at the correct answer. Without challenge, there is no growth. Mistakes can help us to open our minds to new possibilities, take responsibility for our own learning, acquire new skills and strategies, become more resilient in the face of challenges, discover what we are made of, develop sound reasoning, clarify our goals, draw on our creativity and inspire others. They shape our personality and strengthen our character. The mistakes and failures we have protected our children from are the very experiences that teach them how to persist, innovate and become resilient citizens.

Making the most of our mistakes requires us to be open to growth, face our fears and embrace errors as opportunities. By building trusting relationships, we allow ourselves, and teach our students how, to become vulnerable and resilient enough to reflect on:

- where in the process we went wrong;
- our stores of knowledge and strategies ('What Works When'); and
- the skills, knowledge, resources or tools that will help us grow from that error.

What would it look like if we normalised 'not knowing' in our classrooms?

Think about some of your students who appear to make the same error over and over again. How deeply have you probed their metacognitive awareness about themselves as unique learners and their common mistakes? If you asked your students "What is a mistake?", what would they share? It is helpful to develop consensus in your class about defining mistakes in a way that minimises negative language and, at the same time, promotes responsibility for learning. It also helps to clarify that it is not a mistake if we intentionally did something that we knew in advance would result in a negative outcome. It is only a mistake if it has unexpected results.

How do you use incentives such as praise? Do you typically give incentives to the students who get the right answers or 'exceed expectations' OR do you give incentives to the students who demonstrate sound thinking, show ingenuity, take risks and make mistakes and learn from them? Imagine a schoolwide assembly with students sharing where they messed up and receiving awards for what they learned from it. How might that change a student's mindset about what they are capable of?

Think also about the students who are not yet trusting enough to reveal their vulnerabilities around 'not knowing'. Set yourself a classroom culture challenge. Take one week and find out how your students respond when you shift your priorities away from speed, accuracy and quantity to valuing mistakes, struggle and 'not knowing'. What happens when you show enthusiasm when students identify what they don't know? Collect data with your students throughout the week and at the end of the week reflect on:

- what the classroom looked like, felt like and sounded like;
- whether or not they noticed any difference in the way they approached their work; and
- whether or not they felt more comfortable identifying and sharing what they don't know.

Remember Kathy Hannun from the start of this chapter? Her project, Fog Horn, failed and yet Kathy emerged from that experience feeling like an even more capable and confident Rapid Evaluator. She was given a bonus because her evaluation of the project was sound. Also, X celebrated her project at an annual ceremony to recognise the people who had the wisdom to hit the kill switch because, even if the project wasn't the breakthrough they hoped for, *time and resources were still well spent.* They acknowledged what X gained from the lessons learned throughout the project and how X benefited from taking part in the process. This culture at X normalised failure and made it possible to think positively about things that didn't work out. X understood that if you punish failure and you simultaneously know it's inevitable then you create an environment where people are inclined to hide it or misrepresent their work. X supported employees to separate 'I'm a failure' from 'this idea isn't going to work' which are very different things, but don't always feel very different.

(Grant 2021)

How does this example of Kathy and her work with X help you to think differently about the values you are embedding in the culture in your classroom?

Flexible Mindsets language

Our language in the classroom is one of the most powerful ways to create trusting relationships where learners feel comfortable to ask questions, make mistakes and take risks for learning. Language is more than simply expressing thoughts and feelings. What we say and how we say it matters. Our language shapes our sense of self, helps us to understand the world around us and influences all of our interactions. Relationships are built and sustained through the use of language (see Figure 4.3).

Direct, kind and affirmative language is *authentic*. Say what you mean and mean what you say. Give students clear messages and follow through on what you say

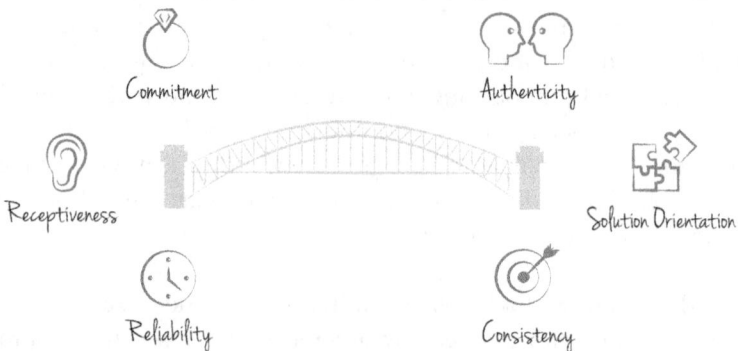

Figure 4.3 Flexible Mindsets language that builds trust

with your actions. Speak the truth, even when doing so is uncomfortable. Avoid couching instructions in questions. This can create an illusion that there is choice, leaving students feeling cheated when there is no choice. For example, avoid sarcasm such as "What did we say about what to do when you're stuck?" Instead shift to language that removes judgement and builds trust for students to take risks for learning.

> "Remember, when you're stuck, you can try switching to a different problem and come back to this one later or you can ask for help to figure out what steps you know and what you are missing."

Changing our language is not easy. It requires *commitment* and vigilance to notice what our words, tone and body language are communicating and catch ourselves so that we can find another strategy. Stay alert to the reality that students assess our level of commitment based on our words and actions. If you pay attention to how you feel, you may notice that you gravitate toward people who make you feel relaxed and bring a smile to your face. Recognising what we are communicating to students through our body language requires ongoing self-reflection and exploration to discover new and more effective ways to communicate.

Developing our emotion skills is an opportunity to build empathy and deepen our insights about what it feels like to be asked to do hard work, feel uncomfortable and change the way we do something (Brackett 2019). Sharing this process of building your own emotion skills demonstrates that you can listen, be vulnerable and are *receptive* to students.

> "I hear you say you can't and I know this is hard because it is the first time we have learned this. Let's see if we can identify a smaller step you could use to get started."

Let students know that, in your presence, there is someone they can *rely* on. Use body language, tone of voice and words that assure students that, rather than being punitive or dismissive, you are on their side in their learning journey. Notice your tone and express genuine curiosity and affection for students. Modelling how things get easier with repeated practice and how we have persevered when it is challenging, can be a great lesson in itself. Let them know you are vulnerable, too, and that the more you put into learning, the more satisfying the outcome.

> "It can be scary to try something outside of your comfort zone. When I feel uncomfortable, I remind myself that it's okay to feel scared and that some of my best learning has happened when I've worked through my struggles."

Being *consistent* provides a degree of predictability. When our environment is predictable, then we feel safe. The more uncertain the world is, the more we need to reassure our students that our expectations and responses will remain consistent.

Ultimately, if our language is *solution oriented*, we build the relationships that help students to trust us and take risks for learning. Intentionally create and practise phrases that acknowledge challenges and offer specific strategies. This will mark the transition from disciplinarian to facilitator of learning.

> "I notice you're distracted. Let's pick a strategy that will help you regain your focus. You could try thinking of questions to ask related to this topic, take sketchnotes, stretch and move around . . ."

This level of surveillance of your language and actions can be hard work and it may feel uncomfortable. Developing our own emotion skills is a great opportunity to build empathy for our students and deepen our insights about what it feels like to be asked to do hard work, feel uncomfortable and change the way we do something. Table 4.1 may be helpful in getting started.

Partner-centred learning spaces derive from co-creation and sharing power. They happen when leadership commits to a set of values about empowering learners to become self-directed. Here are some possible examples of value statements to adopt and adapt as you see fit. You can use them to guide your interactions and use of language to build trusting relationships with students and transform their mindsets:

- *Relationships* are the cornerstone of engaged classrooms: we believe in *trust, mutual respect* and that we are *all capable* of learning.
- *Equity* occurs when we go beyond the Golden Rule by recognising that not every student has the same needs: we *treat each student not just as we would like to be treated, but as that student needs to be treated.*

- Our *priority* is *growth over grades*: high-stakes testing and other imposed structures can be counterbalanced when we permeate a space with the language and responses that *promote I* CAN *messages*.

Table 4.1 The Flexible Mindsets Spiral of Reflective Learning: opening the window for learning

 **BE METACOGNITIVE**	How will you build your own awareness about how you are feeling in the moment and choosing how you want to respond? Get curious about your emotions and investigate underlying themes around feelings such as disappointment results from unmet expectations, rage is about injustice, and joy is related to reaching a goal. Explore tools such as the RULER approach (rulerapproach.org 2021).
 **MODEL**	How will you demonstrate the value of making mistakes for learning? How can you communicate to your students that if they are learning something new, they shouldn't expect to already have the right answers? "How can you take the results of this test, review the mistakes and use it to do something differently next time?"
 **ASK QUESTIONS AND AFFORD TIME**	How will you ask questions that help you get to know your students better and understand underlying emotions? "What's important to you? Let's find ways that we can explore that through this assignment."
 **USE SHARING AS A SPRINGBOARD**	How will you reduce your students' stress about sharing school-related fears such as asking questions and taking tests? (anonymous chat bar during class, Google docs/forms, Survey Monkey, weekly/monthly celebration sharing things that didn't work and what was learned). "Here's our survey results about things that stress us out at school. What has worked to reduce stress and what else could we try?"
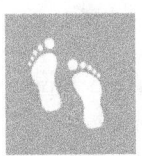 **THINK ON YOUR FEET**	Once you identify a feeling, how will you respond in a way that builds trust? - To yourself, label emotions and underlying reasons. "I'm disappointed because expectations about homework have not been met." - Explain your concerns to the student in a non-judgemental manner. "I notice you haven't submitted your homework again and have not asked for help. Can we work together to find out where the breakdown is happening and brainstorm possible solutions?"

References

Boaler, J. (2010). *The elephant in the classroom: Helping children learn and love maths.* London, UK: Souvenir Press.

Brackett, M. (2019). *Permission to feel: Unlocking the power of emotions to help our kids, ourselves, and our society thrive.* New York, NY: Caledon Books.

Brooks, R. (2015). Resilience: The common underlying factor [online]. *Dr Robert Brooks.* [Viewed 15 August 2020]. Available from: www.drrobertbrooks.com/monthly_articles/resiliencecommonunderlyingfactor

Brooks, R. (2018). Microaffirmations in schools and beyond [online]. *Dr Robert Brooks.* [Viewed 15 August 2020]. Available from: www.drrobertbrooks.com/microaffirmations-in-schools/

Brooks, R. (n.d.). *The power of the relationship and theories of mindset* [online]. [Viewed 13 October 2019]. Available from: www.drrobertbrooks.com/wp/wp-content/uploads/2016/09/Column177-The-Relationship-in-Mindsets.pdf

Dr. Hallowell: Living a better life. (2012). Mrs Eldredge, my first grade teacher [online]. *YouTube.* [Viewed 13 July 2019]. Available from: www.youtube.com/watch?v=7Z6bD4Fz6rY

Duckworth, A., Peterson, C., Matthews, M., & Kelly, D. (2007). Grit: Perseverance and passion for long-term goals. *Journal of Personality and Social Psychology.* **92**(6), 1087–1101.

Duckworth, E. (2006). *"The having of wonderful ideas" and other essays on teaching and learning.* 3rd ed. New York, NY: Teachers College Press.

Dweck, C. (2008). *Mindset: The new psychology of success.* New York, NY: Ballantine.

Grant, A. (2021). How to rethink a bad decision [podcast]. *WorkLife.* [Viewed 2 April 2021]. Available from: https://podcasts.apple.com/us/podcast/how-to-rethink-a-bad-decision/id1346314086?i=1000514966580.

Greene, R. (2014). *Lost at school: Why our kids with behavioral challenges are falling through the cracks and how we can help them.* New York, NY: Scribner.

Hammond, Z. (2015). *Culturally responsive teaching and the brain: Promoting authentic engagement and rigor among culturally and linguistically diverse students.* Thousand Oaks, CA: Corwin.

Maguire, E., Gadian, D., Johnsrude, I., Good, C., Ashburner, J., Frackowiak, R., & Frith, C. (2000). Navigation-related structural change in the hippocampi of taxi drivers. *Proceedings of the National Academy of Sciences of the United States of America* [online]. **97**(8), 4398–4403. [Viewed 2 May 2019]. Available from: doi:10.1073/pnas.070039597

Miller, W., & Rollnick, S. (2013). *Motivational interviewing: Helping people change.* 3rd ed. New York, NY: Guilford Press.

Moser, J., Schroder, H., Heeter, C., Moran, T., & Lee, Y. (2011). Mind your errors: Evidence for a neural mechanism linking growth mind-set to adaptive posterior adjustments. *Psychological Science.* **22**(12), 1484–1489.

Rulerapproach.org. (2021). RULER approach [online]. *Yale University.* [Viewed 8 April 2019]. Available from: www.rulerapproach.org/

Seigal, D., & Bryson, T. (2012). *The whole-brain child: 12 revolutionary strategies to nurture your child's developing mind.* New York, NY: Random House Inc.

Sinek, S. (2009). *Start with why: How great leaders inspire everyone to take action.* New York, NY: Penguin.

Tulis, M., Steuer, G., & Dresel, M. (2016). Learning from errors: A model of individual processes. *Frontline Learning Research* [online]. **4**(4), 12–26. [Viewed 11 April 2019]. Available from: https://files.eric.ed.gov/fulltext/EJ1108798.pdf

CHAPTER 5

The superstructure of Productive Puzzling (conditions 2, 3, 4 and 5)

In Chapter 4, we addressed the first condition necessary for Productive Puzzling: trusting relationships that encourage learning from mistakes, asking questions and taking risks for learning. Chapter 5 addresses the remaining conditions for Productive Puzzling (see Figure 5.1). We discuss:

- the value of practice and struggle for cementing your learning;
- how to teach your students about strategies;
- how to use Carefully Crafted Questions to direct learning towards the 3C's; and
- how to use Flexible Mindsets feedback to help students reflect on strategy use and to persevere.

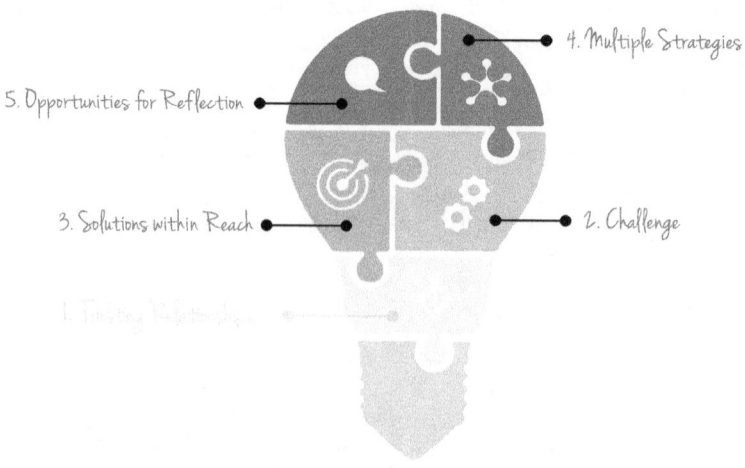

Figure 5.1 The superstructure for Productive Puzzling: conditions 2, 3, 4 and 5

Valuing practice and struggle

In his song "Summer of '69," Bryan Adams describes how he bought his first guitar and played it until his fingers bled. Practice is the most important ingredient in learning, and yet it's often the part we experience the most resistance to because it requires more effort and we mistakenly think practice is optional (Young 2019). Self-directed learners value practice and struggle (condition 2 of Productive Puzzling). They also have found their affinities: those interests and passions that, when we are in the midst of them, engage us to the point that we don't even notice what is happening around us. Engaging in our affinities builds the neural pathways that make us unique and helps us flourish in our natural ways of being. When we discover our affinities, we spontaneously become engrossed in practice, which is the basis for the ongoing process of applying new learning and extending the capacities for Critical Thinking, Complex Problem-Solving and Creativity.

Many students believe that all they need to do to learn is sit in class and listen to their teacher or read their textbook and then they should be able to answer everything on the test. They don't realise – and we don't tell them – that in order to actually learn and retain knowledge, students need to engage with the material and organise it in their brain in a way that makes sense to them. Even when students do try to learn the information on their own, they often use ineffective strategies that don't help the brain process and retain information (Brown, Roediger & McDaniel 2014).

When we are exposed to new material for the first time, it's fine to rely on listening to a lecture or watching a video to jumpstart your learning, but, if we keep doing that, we won't actually be able to take our learning to the next step – application – because we are not solving problems or digging for information on our own. Trial and error is a critical step required to ensure that transfer of learning. Transfer of learning refers to the use of previously acquired knowledge and skills in new learning or problem-solving situations (Steiner 2001). It is the transfer that puts solutions within our reach by helping us to take what we have learned in one context and apply it to a new problem (condition 3 of Productive Puzzling). The most successful learners are students who can identify underlying principles and apply them to new experiences as well as those that can pinpoint critical concepts in a lesson and then link that information to already existing mental structures (Brown, Roediger & McDaniel 2014). This type of ongoing practice takes effort, which students experience as challenge and struggle. It's uncomfortable and they have to focus mental effort in areas that don't hold many short-term rewards. By entwining this struggle with practice, students take incremental steps towards their goals. The value of this type of practice lies in the often unseen and long-term outcomes of cemented learning.

How to teach students about strategies

Productive Puzzling requires students to use effective strategies that are based on current evidence about how the brain learns (condition 4 for Productive Puzzling). These strategies need to be taught purposefully, directly and frequently for students to experience the benefits of studying smarter and appreciate the value of focusing not only on the content of what they are learning but also on how they are learning it. You may have noticed that sometimes we teach a strategy in class, but then students don't apply that strategy when they need it. Our students are no different from us in that we need to see the value of a tool before we use it consistently.

Oftentimes, the missing ingredients are directly teaching students about the brain, how it learns and how to be strategic in their learning. Applying research about the brain, and making it real, helps students to buy into the effort required to learn and apply new strategies. Most students have never been taught how they learn and the strategies they come up with on their own are often not effective. For example, when asked what they think is the best way to study, students will often say reread (review) their notes. Cognitive science research has proven this to be one of the least effective ways to study (Willingham 2009). Gretchen Wegner, an internationally recognised expert, has developed a simple practical system for teaching students the science of learning and strategies to put that science into practice. She trains educators all over the world in her signature course *The Art of Inspiring Students to Study Strategically* (Wegner 2019). This type of system is the bridge we need to teach students how to learn strategically and take ownership of their learning.

In addition to the science of learning, we can teach students how to be metacognitive by engaging in explicit self-examination and exploring which strategies work best for them. This is particularly important for questioning, solving and imagining. Knowing that there are multiple strategies for reaching a goal provides the foundation for Flexible Mindsets: the ability to shift perspectives and adapt while learning. The strategies that work for one learner may be counterproductive for another. Success is finding a system that allows learners to effectively and efficiently find what they need, when they need it. Before they can apply a strategy, learners must have metacognitive knowledge that goes beyond awareness of their own learning profiles. They require direct instruction in understanding which strategies match well to their strengths in solving a particular problem. This starts with making strategy knowledge explicit:

> "Derrick used speech-to-text today to write his paper. Share with the class why you chose to use this strategy for this particular assignment. How did this strategy work for you and what didn't work?"

The more attention you draw to strategies, the more intentional your students can become in thinking about 'What Works When'.

When drawing attention to strategy use, it is important to ensure that your students have a clear and shared definition of the word 'strategy'. In the Flexible Mindsets framework, *strategies* are the *deliberate, goal-directed attempts that require mental effort: they are what we use when we don't know*. Strategies are an integral part of learning: they are the tools that help us learn HOW to learn.

We find that it is most straightforward to teach what a strategy is by modelling, labelling and sharing actual strategies. The more examples you have of strategies, the more you can recognise a strategy. It is also helpful to teach learners what strategies aren't. If I use repeated addition to multiply two single digit numbers, I am using a strategy. If I practise my times tables over and over, I am using a rehearsal strategy. If I automatically 'know' the product of two single digit numbers, I am no longer using a strategy – I have an automatic skill.

Similarly, if we think about the habits of effective learners, something has to happen before they become habits. First, at the metacognitive level, a learner recognises the need for change. We may find ourselves having difficulty remembering important concepts and then recognise that this could be improved by making connections to things we already know. Initially, we will have to use conscious strategies to help us do this. Eventually, after lots of practice, we will no longer actively walk through the steps of a strategy. Making connections will have become a habit.

To unpack the definition of a strategy, use non-academic examples such as those listed in Table 5.1 to consciously think about all the different things they could do to reach a goal. Encourage students to identify additional goals and brainstorm multiple strategies.

Once your students have a clear understanding of what a strategy is, you can begin to expand metacognitive knowledge about strategies using a variety of techniques:

- small and large group discussions (strategy shares);
- bonus questions on assignments and tests that ask students to explain or show the strategy they used for a particular item (Meltzer 2010);
- student-produced strategy models, posters and boards; and
- personalised mindmaps.

All students benefit from knowing WHY we need strategies along with explicit instruction in HOW to use strategies to support their learning. It is our knowledge of strategies, ability to reflect on 'What Works When' and adapt them that leads to self-directed learning.

Table 5.1 Examples of strategies for everyday goals

Goal	Possible strategies
Teach a dog to sit	■ say "sit"; ■ use a hand gesture; ■ press the dog into a sitting position; ■ take the dog to a dog trainer.
Learn to make decorative cakes	■ get guidance from an expert; ■ watch a video clip; ■ follow a recipe; ■ practise, make mistakes, try a different technique.
Answer a question on a game show such as *Millionaire*	■ know and use mental effort to retrieve the answer; ■ phone a friend; ■ ask the audience; ■ 50/50 (narrow the choices).

Carefully Crafted Questions for exploring the 3C's

Self-reflection is pivotal for giving students agency over their own learning (condition 5 for Productive Puzzling). The right questions are the pathway to self-directed learning. Classrooms are often filled with questions. In fact, asking questions is the second most common instructional practice, with the most common practice being lecturing (Black 2001). Despite the popularity of questions in the classroom, they are often used for simple recall of facts or as a review of material covered (e.g., summarise the lesson). They are rarely used to spark curiosity, develop deeper thinking skills and encourage self-reflection.

We can't think critically, solve complex problems or be creative without asking the right questions. Instead of mapping questions onto content, we can set learning objectives around the 3 C's and integrate content into learning activities.

Question taxonomies are helpful in thinking strategically about what you are asking students to do and ensuring that a variety of questions are being asked to target different levels of thinking and reflection about strategies. They are also helpful for students to guide the types of questions they ask both in classroom discussions as well as when they are studying. In the Flexible Mindsets model, Carefully Crafted Questions are grounded in questioning taxonomies. In education there are ongoing discussions about whether it is necessary to build factual knowledge prior to developing higher order thinking. Bloom's taxonomy is a widely used model that classifies thinking hierarchically (Bloom 1956). This taxonomy has been revised to include the use of verbs to describe increasingly complex types of thinking (Anderson et al. 2001). As an example, let's consider the ancient tale of "The Lion and the Mouse."

> A Lion lay asleep in the forest, his great head resting on his paws. A timid little Mouse came upon him unexpectedly, and in her fright and haste to get away, ran across the Lion's nose. Roused from his nap, the Lion laid his huge paw on the tiny creature to kill her.
>
> "Spare me!" begged the poor Mouse. "Please let me go and someday I will surely repay you." The Lion was much amused to think that a Mouse could ever help him. But he was generous and finally let the Mouse go.
>
> Some days later, while stalking his prey in the forest, the Lion was caught in a hunter's net. Unable to free himself, he let out a roar that echoed throughout the forest. The Mouse knew the voice and quickly found the Lion struggling in the net. Running to one of the great ropes that bound him, she gnawed it until it frayed and soon the Lion was free.
>
> "You laughed when I said I would repay you," said the Mouse. "Now you see that even a Mouse can help a Lion."

Remember:	What did the lion do when the mouse ran across his nose?
Understand:	Why did the lion think that a mouse could never help a lion?
Apply:	Who do you know who might think that you could never help them? Why would people think that you are not able to help them?
Analyse:	What would the story be like if it was about the Horse and the Sparrow?
Evaluate:	In this story, who do you think had more power: the lion or the mouse? Explain your reasoning.
Create:	Write a story about yourself where you might need help from someone and then have the chance to help that person later on.

While Bloom's taxonomy is often presented as progressing from factual knowledge through analysis and creation, with Flexible Mindsets, there is not a unidirectional flow of learning. A taxonomy does not have to be hierarchical in nature; it is a classification system. More recent research has questioned whether lower order knowledge must precede higher order thinking or if in fact the more complex instructional techniques utilised during higher order thinking tasks might actually improve student engagement and therefore promote deeper learning (Agarwal 2019).

Productive Puzzling is a definitive example of the type of higher order thinking that stimulates student's minds by piquing their curiosity, engrossing them in challenges that interest them enough to discover what they don't know and engaging them in self-reflection.

Metacognitively, it is important to know one's learning goal and to match it to the appropriate type of question: "Do you want to know specific facts about a

Productive Puzzling conditions

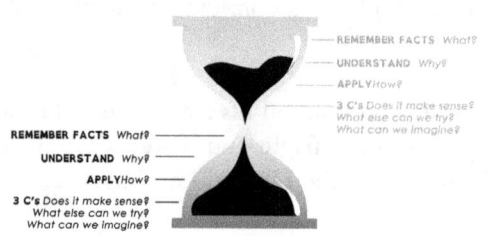
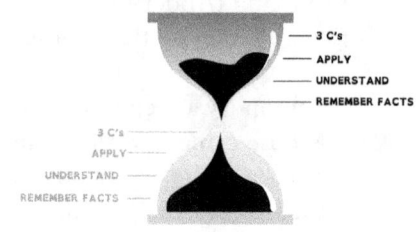

Figure 5.2 The Flexible Mindsets bidirectional questioning taxonomy

topic? Are you interested in exploring ideas around a topic or maybe you want to develop your own opinion on the topic? Do you have a complex problem to solve that requires multiple types of questions?" Flexible learners move fluidly back and forth between the different types of questions. As such, Flexible Mindsets conceptualises our taxonomy as a set of question types that each address different learning goals. When engaged in Critical Thinking, Complex Problem-Solving and Creativity, learners shift constantly between these types of questions and don't have to start in a predetermined place. This fluidity in questioning deepens Productive Puzzling, helps students identify the next step in their learning and extends their ability to be self-directed.

In Figure 5.2, the hourglass image is used to illustrate our bidirectional questioning taxonomy. The Flexible Mindsets model accentuates the value of shifting between a variety of question types, with differing emphasis, depending on the learning goal.

The types of questions we prioritise are linked directly to the metacognitive learning goal (adapted from The LearnWell Projects n.d.):

- identify/define: *What is . . . ? When did . . . ? Who are . . . ?*
- understand: *Why is . . . ? Why did . . . ? Explain the similarities/differences between . . .*
- Apply: *How can . . . ? How many ways can we . . . ? How does this apply to . . . ?*
- The 3C's: *Does it make sense? What else can we try? What are the possibilities?*

The grains of learning can flow from knowledge to capacities such as the 3C's. At any point during the learning process, the hourglass can be inverted such that the grains flow from higher order capacities to help learners fill in the conceptual and factual details.

Asking and answering Carefully Crafted Questions is a well-honed skill. We are not born knowing how to ask and answer good questions, so we have to meet students where they are. Some students will come from a home where dinner time is conversational and includes thought-provoking questions. Other students may have very little exposure to questions. Here are some of our tips for teaching students HOW to ask, listen and respond to questions:

- Start with discussing questions in general and what students know about asking good questions. For example, it starts with a genuine curiosity about the answer, rather than just trying to show what you already know.
- Clarify the difference between statements, closed and open-ended questions as well as reflective questions.
- Provide initial instruction on what the different types of questions are and how to respond to questions thoughtfully and fully. Clearly identify the type of question you are asking before you ask (i.e., understanding, applying, etc.) and remind students that they can expand their learning by asking themselves different types of questions that access different types of thinking.
- Often students will rush to answer questions without first stopping to think about what the question is really asking and how they want to respond. Classrooms breed quick and simple responses as students compete with each other to be the first to respond. One way to change this dynamic is to model 'thinking time' when you respond to student questions and, correspondingly, implement a wait time before any hands can go up.

(Wilson 2015)

> "I'm going to take a moment to think about that and then respond."

Flexible Mindsets feedback: perseverance PLUS flexible strategy use

Feedback is the vehicle for self-reflection (condition 5). When feedback is born in a fixed mentality culture, it leaves little room for growth towards self-directed learning. It consciously or unconsciously disempowers students and reinforces myths about abilities and getting the 'right' answer. In this section, we will review:

1. the use of metacognitive feedback and mistakes to help students identify what they do and don't know;
2. how feedback should be rooted in growth mindsets (with a caveat about effort); and
3. the priority of focusing feedback on flexible strategy use.

You may have encountered something like the following example:

> Mr Findlay is an experienced teacher and an astute observer of children's skills and behaviours. Within the first week or two of school, he has spotted those children who will follow the rules, answer questions and coast through the year. He has also identified those children who will easily become frustrated, seem confused and, if pushed, may act out. As he delivers content, he often calls on Devrae who always has the correct answer. Millie never raises her hand, but there are times when Mr Findlay calls on her. In these rare instances, Millie produces a huge yawn and rests her head on her desk. Mr Findlay's comments to Devrae are frequent, yet brief: "Great job!" or "That's brilliant" or "I expect great things from you." In Millie's case, Mr Findlay's feedback is different: "Keep on trying!" or "You'll need to put in more effort" or "Let's find a study buddy to help you practise more."

Although there is nothing wrong with Mr Findlay's feedback, it does communicate fixed mentality messages to his students. Devrae is 'intelligent' because he can memorise stuff easily, doesn't have to try hard and finishes his work quickly. Conversely, Millie is 'less smart' because she has to try really hard to pass. Unfortunately, because she has been given the message that she is not capable and fears the humiliation of trying and still failing, she has disengaged from the learning process and her window for learning is closing.

Metacognition and mistakes

When delivered well, feedback can be a powerful tool to develop students' agency in directing their own learning. However, learning from feedback does not come naturally to students. Coaching students to think about what the feedback means and asking them what they can do differently next time helps them become more independent with this skill over time. The words you use when giving feedback are particularly important. Minimise approval-seeking feeling words such as "I like . . ." when sharing feedback with students. Avoid telling a student "I like the way you started your story." Instead be specific about the technique or strategy they used.

> "You started your story with a fascinating question that made me want to read more. This is a great technique for hooking your audience."

The same holds true for constructive feedback. State what the student needs to address without expressing any disappointment. Don't say, "You used so many similes in your story that I lost interest." Take yourself out of the equation by describing the impact that a particular strategy has when it is underused, overused or misused.

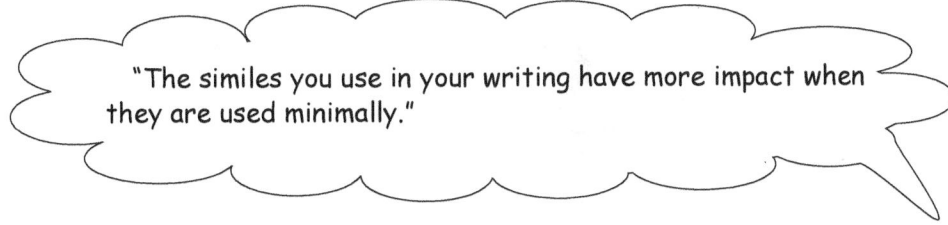

"The similes you use in your writing have more impact when they are used minimally."

Focus on the skills you want to build in students and not on your feelings or reactions to them.

Feedback based on growth-mindset messages

The research on growth mindsets (Dweck 2008) and grit (Duckworth 2016) can liberate us from the misinformed constraints of viewing abilities as fixed. Now that we know that brains can grow, we no longer need to limit children's beliefs about intelligence. Brains can get smarter. "You have to try hard because you aren't smart" becomes "You are capable and trying flexibly makes your brain grow."

Many schools provide feedback, and even assign grades, to their students based on their effort. A word of caution: tying success and failure primarily to effort has its limitations for several reasons:

- Effort is inherently difficult to measure. It can't be objectively seen. A student's self-rating of his or her effort may differ drastically from the teacher's perspective. Whilst this discrepancy can be used to help students and teachers to work towards a common definition of effort, it cannot stand alone as an intervention (SMARTS 2003).
- Effort is exhaustible. If a student has used up buckets of mental energy to get this far, more effort may not be viable. Over decades of working with students who learn differently, we have repeatedly heard that 'keep trying' can discourage many children whose families and teachers have had the best of intentions.
- Effort alone is not always the answer. Practising the same incorrect method guarantees that we will get it wrong.
- When we refer *solely* to the effort of the student, we let ourselves off the hook from direct confrontation of systemic inequities. This can manifest as a form of coded language that acts as an indirect expression of victim blaming.

Flexible Mindsets feedback: perseverance PLUS flexible strategy use

Flexible Mindsets differ from growth mindsets in that we encourage attributions to the combination of both strategy use and perseverance. *Perseverance is the determination to keep working towards a goal in the absence of an external reward.*

Reflecting on effort (*How hard did you try?*) is subject to a multitude of interpretations and can fail to effect change. In contrast, feedback becomes powerful when

Productive Puzzling conditions

Figure 5.3 Perseverance PLUS flexible strategy use equals resilience and adaptability

it encourages the learner to reflect one's own perseverance and use of strategies (see Figure 5.3): How long did I keep going? How many attempts did I make? How many *different strategies* did I try?

I can keep going *and* try something new.

We often encourage students to 'work smarter, not harder'. But we know that self-directed learning involves both working harder and smarter. We need to unpack these terms for students. What does it mean to work 'smarter'? It means that, yes, we need to persevere when we learn, and, at the same time, we can do this in a way that is effective and doesn't waste our time.

Similar to the work of Dr Lynn Meltzer and her team (Meltzer 2010; SMARTS 2003), the Flexible Mindsets shift towards prioritising strategy feedback places the power to learn within the grasp of our students. It can also inform the model we use when teaching students to deliver feedback to each other. In addition to developing shared ground rules for trusting relationships, students can be taught to refer specifically to strategies when giving and receiving feedback. They can practise using phrases and questions such as: "What strategies did you try? How did they work or not work? It looks as if your [question, plan, mindmap, note taking, research strategy] was helpful. What advice would you give to other students who will be attempting this type of project/test/essay?"

> "Don't forget to hand in your exit slips. I want to know: How did you study? Did it help? What didn't help? What will you add to your study strategies next time? You will get bonus points for handing in your exit slip."

Transforming mindsets requires Metacognitive Insights and effective strategies. Let's return to Mr Findlay as he changes the mindset culture in his classroom . . .

Mr Findlay is now calling on a wider range of students: when he calls on students like Devrae, he is asking appropriately challenging questions that target analysis and application; for students like Millie, he is asking questions about facts and concepts that are directly related to an area of interest to each individual student. His feedback to students is consistent and conveys confidence in all students to learn. He uses questions that provoke reflection such as "I noticed that you spent a lot of time on your essay: what helped you to organise your thoughts?" "I see that you looked for and corrected your mistakes. How did that work for you?" "During our class discussion, I observed many of you listening to feedback and thinking about how you can use different strategies for improving your work. What are your takeaways?"

In a Flexible Mindsets environment, reflection is encouraged by targeting feedback at strategy use and perseverance. As opposed to effort only, strategies are specific enough that they can be measured, worked on and used to track progress. We define *Flexible Mindsets feedback* as *responses that are targeted at specific strategies, solution oriented, empathetic and encourage trying a different approach to a problem*. As the final condition for Productive Puzzling, reflection is a tool for both evaluating progress and pointing you towards directing your own learning. Please refer to Table 5.2 for ideas that target Flexible Mindsets feedback.

Table 5.2 The Flexible Mindsets Spiral of Reflective Learning: the superstructure of Productive Puzzling

 **BE METACOGNITIVE**	Review your feedback to students. Looking holistically at a student's responses, what common error patterns can you identify? How will you communicate these in relation to strategy use?
	When a student struggles, take the time one on one to point this out to and help him/her personalise the strategy that works best for him/her.
	Reframe feedback to focus more on strategy use. "I see that Nahzai added 5 + 3 by counting up from 5. Ryley used the number line. I wonder what else we could use for adding . . . ?"
 **MODEL**	How will you share how you have grappled with how to teach your students new content?
	How will you model the ways that you set goals you can reach, challenge yourself and respond to setbacks?
 **ASK QUESTIONS AND AFFORD TIME**	Choose a learning goal and decide how you will use a variety of Carefully Crafted Questions. Use a provocation to elicit a Metacognitive Insight where students recognise that some questions are about knowledge and others help us go deeper into a topic by asking questions using *What? Why?* and *How?*

Table 5.2 (Continued)

 **USE SHARING AS A SPRINGBOARD**	What additional techniques for strategy sharing will you use to encourage students to reflect on, and give and receive feedback, about strategy use and perseverance? Have strategy shares such as small group discussions about the strategies students are using that work and don't work for them.
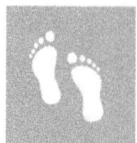 **THINK ON YOUR FEET**	How will you use Carefully Crafted Questions to resist the temptation to 'rescue' students? Adapt the work on Productive Struggle (Warshauer 2015): 1 Take the pressure off: "What do you know about this . . . ?" 2 Probe: "What strategies have you tried so far? What else could you try?" 3 Allow some time for puzzling. 4 Guide: "Tell me again about your goal and what isn't working. I wonder what would happen if you tried . . . ?"

References

Agarwal, P. (2019). Retrieval practice & Bloom's taxonomy: Do students need fact knowledge before higher order learning? *Journal of Educational Psychology.* **111**(2), 189–209.

Anderson, L., Krathwohl, D., Airasian, P., Cruikshank, K., Mayer, R., Pintrich, P., & Wittrock, M. (2001). *A taxonomy for learning, teaching, and assessing: A revision of Bloom's taxonomy of educational objectives.* Abridged ed. New York, NY: Addison Wesley Longman.

Black, S. (2001). Ask me a question: How teachers use inquiry in the classroom. *American School Board Journal.* **188**(5), 43–45.

Bloom, B. (1956). *Taxonomy of educational objectives, handbook I: Cognitive domain.* New York, NY: David McKay.

Brown, P., Roediger, H., & McDaniel, M. (2014). *Make it stick: The science of successful learning.* Cambridge, MA: The Belknap Press of Harvard University Press.

Duckworth, A. (2016). *Grit: The power of passion and perseverance.* New York, NY: Simon & Schuster.

Dweck, C. (2008). *Mindset: The new psychology of success.* New York, NY: Ballantine.

The LearnWell Projects. (n.d.). ThinkWell-LearnWell Diagram [online]. *The LearnWell Projects.* [Viewed 25 August 2020]. Available from: https://thelearnwellprojects.com/resources/

Meltzer, L. (2010). *Promoting executive function in the classroom*. New York, NY: Guilford Press.

SMARTS. (2003). MetaCOG: Metacognitive Awareness Assessment System [online]. *RESEARCHILD*. Available from: https://smarts-ef.org/executivefunction packages/metacog-metacognitive-awareness-assessment-system/

Steiner, G. (2001). Transfer of learning, cognitive psychology of. *International Encyclopedia of the Social & Behavioral Sciences*. **15**, 845–851.

Warshauer, H. (2015). Productive struggle in middle school mathematics classrooms. *Journal of Mathematics Teacher Education*. **17**(4), 375–400.

Wegner, G. (2019). The study cycle 101. Gretchen Wegner [online]. *Gretchen Wegner*. [Viewed 18 February 2020]. Available from: https://gretchenwegner.com/study-cycle-101-live-masterclass-winter-2019/

Willingham, D. (2009). *Why don't students like school? A cognitive scientist answers questions about how the mind works and what it means for your classroom*. New York, NY: Wiley.

Wilson, M. (2015). *The language of learning: Teaching students core thinking, listening and speaking skills*. Turner Falls, MA: Center for Responsive Schools, Inc.

Young, S. (2019). *Ultralearning: Master hard skills, outsmart the competition, and accelerate your career*. New York, NY: HarperCollins.

SECTION

Productive Puzzling in action

How do we target the 3C's?

Now is the time to ask "Where are we in the journey of this book and beyond?"

In Section I we introduced the definition of Flexible Mindsets as the adaptive strategy use and perseverance that constitute the journey of self-directed learning. We illustrated the role of curiosity in activating the brain, and defined Productive Puzzling as the mechanism that drives Flexible Mindsets.

In Section II we focused on the conditions for Productive Puzzling. Chapters 3 and 4 started with condition 1: the importance of trusting relationships. In Chapter 5, we reiterated the importance of conditions 2 and 3, balancing challenge and attainable solutions by highlighting the value of practice and struggle. Chapter 5 also laid out the how-to's for meeting conditions 4 and 5: multiple strategies and reflection. These include how to teach students about strategies, using Carefully Crafted Questions and targeting feedback with a combination of flexible strategy use and perseverance. We now have all the building blocks we need to empower our students to direct their learning journeys.

Here in Section III we will pull everything together and apply Productive Puzzling to Critical Thinking, Complex Problem-Solving and Creativity. Later, we briefly highlight the criteria for Flexible Mindsets strategies and present a table that summarises their application to the 3C's. Chapters 6, 7 and 8 will elaborate on, and offer practical examples for, using Flexible Mindsets to bring the 3C's to life.

Criteria for Flexible Mindsets strategies

Based on our model, we define a Flexible Mindsets strategy as one that meets the following criteria. They:

- can be taught metacognitively to deepen knowledge about 'What Works When';
- engage students in Productive Puzzling;

- reflect current evidence from the science of learning;
- can be applied to multiple content areas; and
- can be adapted to apply at different stages of development.

Section III Introduction Table 1 summarises the 3C's and outlines Chapters 6, 7 and 8.

The 3<u>C</u>'s in action

Section III Introduction Table 1: Flexible Mindsets summary of the 3<u>C</u>'s

	Ch 6: <u>C</u>ritical Thinking	Ch 7: <u>C</u>omplex Problem-Solving	Ch 8: <u>C</u>reativity
Keyword	*Question*	*Solve*	*Imagine*
Symbol			
Target Question	*Does it make sense?*	*What else can we try?*	*What are the possibilities?*
Tool	*Criteria*	*Shifting Perspectives*	*Novelty*
Strategy 1	*Is! Is Not!*	*Mix Master*	*Bending, Breaking or Blending*
Strategy 2	*Prove it!*	*Fork in the Road*	*Diffuse Dreams*
Strategy 3	*Grapple to Grasp*	*Mind Reminder*	*Crazy Connections*

Teaching the 3<u>C</u>'s requires schools to undergo the transformation from fixed mentalities to Flexible Mindsets. Educators will need the 3<u>C</u>'s to teach the 3<u>C</u>'s. This reconstruction is grounded in our capacities to empathise, struggle, grapple, puzzle, change our habits and persevere. By embodying Flexible Mindsets, we empower our students to chart their own course and embrace the endless adventure of self-directed learning.

CHAPTER

Critical Thinking
Does it make sense?

"Education is not the learning of facts, but training the mind to think."

(Albert Einstein)

As we write this book, the globe is facing unprecedented challenges. People from some countries are looking at other countries and saying, "What were you thinking?" Many people are also looking at their own countries and saying, "How did we get here?" We argue that many of these circumstances have arisen from people who blindly follow ideology, people who fear repercussions and don't feel they are in a position to challenge the system, and the privileged people who have no incentive to change the status quo. Simply put, we need to do a better job of teaching everyone HOW to think rather than WHAT to think and ask the question *Does it make sense?*

Let's think about a headline we might see that says, *Veterans are better off than they were two years ago.* Do we want to merely believe this position or should we verify the factual basis for the statement? The article supports its argument by saying that there are more veterans enrolling in social programmes and that there are fewer opioids being prescribed for veterans. Does this convince you? How would you investigate? What would you consider to be reliable sources for your research? What would you use to sift through the mountains of available data? If you came across figures showing that the suicide rate amongst veterans is significantly higher than it was two years ago, then what would you think?

How good are we at questioning and being questioned? Thought-provoking questions lie at the heart of Productive Puzzling. It is inquisitive minds that lead to thoughtful analysis, social change, entrepreneurship and innovation. If we are to adequately prepare people to think critically, we must teach them how to ask questions that predispose them to think in what-ifs and to use both ethical and deductive reasoning. To do this, the focus in education needs to shift from teaching students what to think to teaching students how to think. Educators need to be comfortable with encouraging struggle and asking provocative questions that challenge the status quo.

Critical Thinking is not just critiquing and decision making; it is about exploring ideas in greater depth. It is closely aligned with definitions of elaboration such as "the process of finding additional layers of meaning" (Brown, Roediger & McDaniel 2014). Without asking *Does this make sense?*, the civil rights movement would never have existed; Galileo would never have concluded that the Earth moves around the sun; and ancient Africans would not have built the pyramids, forged the earliest known peace treaty or made dramatic advancements in mathematics, medicine, agriculture and metallurgy. Critical Thinking is a mode of thinking that can be applied to any situation, from identifying counterfeit money to reducing our carbon footprint to legislative change. We need to develop the mental habit of questioning and to use it all the time. Without it, our minds become suggestible and vulnerable to misinformation (see Figure 6.1).

In this chapter, we will:

1 define Critical Thinking as it relates to Flexible Mindsets;
2 briefly illustrate how questions help the brain learn;
3 describe three strategies for asking and answering the question *Does it make sense?*;
4 share an example of a teacher using Productive Puzzling to engage students in Critical Thinking and reinforce Flexible Mindsets; and
5 present items from the Flexible Learning Activation Checklist (FLAC) to track your progress in creating an environment that feeds Critical Thinking.

Figure 6.1 Critical Thinking: *Does it make sense?*

Flexible Mindsets definition of Critical Thinking

Critical Thinking is the capacity that is built through the habit of independent thinking using reasoning, discernment and empathy to analyse issues, decisions, questions and problems. It requires the ability to keep an open mind, be inquisitive and apply strategies to think systematically. In Flexible Mindsets, we focus on using strategies to help us make meaning, dive deeply into concepts and arrive at judgements. Critical thinkers strive to:

- question from a place of curiosity and be aware that things are not always as they might appear;
- build the habit of noticing juxtapositions, paradoxes, contradictions and other things that don't make sense;
- be receptive to information that contradicts their opinions and flexible enough to change their minds;
- appreciate the complexity of issues and avoid taking a simplistic view of what is being learned;
- be aware of their own biases, prejudices and self-interests;
- acknowledge that thinking is inherently flawed with mistakes and that thoughts are often irrational;
- be grounded in a strong set of ethics and principles that drive them to question whether or not something is fair or just and to stand up for their beliefs;
- follow the logic of an argument and recognise claims that warrant further evaluation;
- weigh up the pros and cons to make a decision or draw a conclusion; and
- back up a position so that it makes sense to others.

It is only through the tools of Critical Thinking that learners can be empowered to give themselves permission to question authority, judge the credibility of sources and trust themselves to evaluate options and act. By overrepresenting knowledge as absolutely correct or incorrect, we deny students the opportunity to make sense of our constantly shifting world and its complexities. Self-directed learners continuously develop the habit of using strategies to explore information from different perspectives, with the goal of improving our world and contributing to a more balanced and equitable society.

Most curricula gloss over important strategies that help students to juggle, sort, discern and appraise. Critical Thinking is what distinguishes unjustified beliefs from informed opinions. Irrespective of the topic, any commentary can be met with *Does it make sense?* Am I going to believe this or not? Is this fair or just? Why or why not?"

How do questions help the brain learn?

Have you ever noticed that when someone asks you a question, you become preoccupied with it and can't concentrate properly on anything else? Research in neuroscience has found that the human brain can only think about one idea at a time. Even when we think we are multitasking, our brains are biologically wired to pay attention to one thing at a time to maximise our chances of survival (Medina 2008). When questions are posed, our whole brain is stimulated and serotonin is released. This release allows the brain to relax and search for information to answer the question. As we prepare to respond, there will be a release of dopamine which can either help or hinder our ability to reason. The dopamine can trigger our reward system and motivate us to search for the answer or, if we are afraid of getting the wrong answer, it can stifle our ability to think. Either way, our 'fight flight freeze' response will trigger a reflex called instinctive elaboration in which our brains are unable to contemplate anything other than the answer to the question (Cooper 2018; Hoffeld 2017). Questions ignite a level of focus that is unmatched by any other type of input. As we consider how to shift our focus from teaching to co-learning, questions become one of the most powerful tools for promoting self-directed learning.

Metacognition applied to Critical Thinking

Each of us has a theory of knowledge. Critical Thinking is about developing methodologies that help us to judge the validity of our learning and to broaden its scope. More than any previous generation, today's students are besieged by information overload. The rapid advancement of artificial intelligence means that we are often one step behind on techniques for dealing with issues such as the impact of deep fake videos and disinformation campaigns. Our increasing comfort with humanoids, if not counterbalanced, may lead us to cede too much power to technology that is not capable of the intuitive leaps and empathy that are the essence of being human.

Before introducing specific strategies for Critical Thinking, it is important for students to examine their own strengths and weaknesses in terms of the degree to which they accept without questioning. Start by brainstorming and coming up with shared definitions of both knowledge and Critical Thinking. Then invite your students to consider questions such as: "Are there some people I believe or follow more than others? Do I fact check what I read on the internet? When does it make sense to take a leap of faith? What are the underlying moral principles that guide my actions? How often do I look at an issue from multiple viewpoints? How often do I ask someone to back up what he or she is saying?" Once they have explored these questions, help students identify their personal strengths and

Table 6.1 Metacognitive Insights Survey (MIS): Critical Thinking

Critical Thinking item	Yes 😊	Sort of 😐	Not Yet ☹
I notice contradictions and other things that don't make sense			
I know my biases and prejudices			
I am open and flexible about changing my mind			
I can follow the logic of someone else's argument			
When making decisions, I weigh up the pros and cons of something			
I back up my opinions using facts and reasoning			
My beliefs are consistent with human rights and social justice			
. . .			

weaknesses in terms of Critical Thinking. You may recall from Chapter 1 that the Metacognitive Insights Survey (MIS) is a component of our Flexible Learning Environmental Scan (FLES). For some sample items from the MIS, please refer to Table 6.1 and Appendix B.

Remember, Critical Thinking is the means by which you can help students to be okay with uncertainty, appreciate the views of others, develop tolerance for disagreement and find common ground. As we promote Flexible Mindsets, it is important to convey to students that we don't know everything. Our goal is not to know everything, but to develop the Metacognitive Insights and executive function strategies that help us learn HOW to learn. If we are comfortable with the notion that everyone falls prey to faulty reasoning, then we have the freedom to change our minds and hearts and to improve our decision making.

Flexible Mindset strategies for Critical Thinking

In a recent Stanford University study with 3,446 high school students across the United States (Wineburg et al. 2020), students evaluated a range of videos, websites, articles and social media claims. In one task, students were asked to evaluate whether or not a particular website was a reliable source of information about climate change. They were reminded that they were allowed to search online to answer that question. A simple search revealed that the website is run by the Center for the Study of Carbon Dioxide and Global Change, a nonprofit organisation funded by fossil fuel companies that are invested in downplaying the impact of climate change. More than 96% of students surveyed failed to consider that ties to the fossil fuel industry might affect the credibility of the website.

Today's students are speeding along the information highway without a driver's license. *Does this make sense?*

By teaching these Critical Thinking strategies directly, our children will learn to question. Through repetitive exposure across the lifespan, by doing these things over and over, we are laying the foundation for habits of thinking. These habits lay the groundwork for adaptability and resilience for today's unexpected events and the uncertainties of tomorrow.

Your main tool for promoting Critical Thinking is using criteria to answer the question *Does it make sense?* Critical Thinking begins with noticing when information doesn't make sense and seizing upon that moment to delve deeper. This applies, not only to the questions you ask, but also to the ones students ask themselves and others. Strategies for Critical Thinking include reverse engineering, analogies, prioritisation, evaluations and a variety of mindmaps (compare and contrast, categorise, part-whole relationships, cause and effect). The commonality found in these types of strategies is that they provide a framework for students to uncover the structure of information and to make it visible. When students can identify the structure of the information, they can then work with it, move it around and discover what they know and what they don't know. This is the essence of how you figure out *Does it make sense?* In the next section, we review three strategies that are most closely aligned with Production Puzzling:

Strategy #1: *Is! Is Not!* Examples and counterexamples to dive deeply into concepts

Strategy #2: *Prove it!* Criteria for arriving at judgements/justifying a position

Strategy #3: *Grapple to Grasp* Retrieval practice for making meaning

Strategy #1: *Is! Is Not!*
(Examples and counterexamples to delve deeper into concepts)

Getting the 'right' answers quickly does not support conceptual understanding. If we focus solely on getting the right answers, we don't achieve true understanding or depth of knowledge. We all know intuitively that it is easier to understand concepts if we provide examples and counterexamples. But how do we teach students to use this strategy independently to learn HOW to learn?

Direct strategy instruction at the whole class level begins with the metacognitive understanding of 'What Works When'. Next we share a simple example that has been used with college students and can be used at all ages to teach students how to think about using examples and counterexamples to explore concepts:

***Is! Is Not!* Example 1:** What is a ball?

You can introduce this strategy by using a simple example of the concept of a 'ball'. Bring a variety of balls to class (e.g., tennis, squash, cricket, baseball, beachball).

Step 1 Examples: One at a time, throw the balls to different students and have the class state what each one is. Ask the students to label the category of objects (balls) and brainstorm the *criteria* that makes something a ball (spherical, can be thrown, etc.).

Step 2 Exceptions: Throw out a ball that violates the criteria such as an American football. Have the students call out *Is!* or *Is Not!*. Ensure they go back to the criteria and ask "Does it make sense that this is a ball?" Challenge them as to the accuracy of their criteria. Do they need to add a criterion such as 'used for sports', delete or revise criteria or add exceptions to the rule?

Step 3 Counterexamples: Throw out a counterexample that closely resembles a ball (e.g., orange) provoke the class by saying "Is this a ball? I say it *Is!*" Prime the students to say "*Is Not!*" and ask them why not. Again, have them review the criteria and amend as needed.

Step 4 Definition: Finally, have them write a definition of 'ball' and compare it to definitions from other sources.

The takeaway from this activity is to help students understand the value of thinking critically about concepts by understanding how to apply criteria to assess claims and to be open to trying this strategy on a number of topics.

***Is! Is Not!* Example 2:** What does the word 'flexible' mean? Are numbers 'flexible'?

This activity can be used to deepen understanding of concepts across all content areas. Choose a vocabulary word that you want your students to understand so they can apply it to Critical Thinking. Here is an example that we have used to teach vocabulary.

Step 1 Examples: Provide images that show different representations of the meaning of 'flexible' (bendy straw, person touching toes, plan A and plan B, forest for trees, multiple word meanings, turning a boot into a planter). Next, have the students make a list of criteria for determining whether or not something is flexible.

Step 2 Exceptions: Ask the students to say whether whole numbers belong in the *Is!* category or the *Is Not!* category and have them call out their answers. Facilitate a discussion about how numbers can be seen as inflexible because their value never changes. Yet they can also be considered to be flexible because they can be expressed in so many different ways. Have them decide whether or not to revise their criteria for the concept of 'flexible'.

Step 3 Counterexamples: provide a set of pictures where some are examples and some are counterexamples representing flexibility. Have the students sort them into two groups of pictures: the *Is!* category and the *Is Not!* category. Again, have them revise the criteria as needed.

Step 4 Definition: Finally, have them write a definition of 'flexible' and compare it to definitions from other sources.

Ensure that you facilitate student reflection on the difference between reading a definition in a textbook versus using the *Is! Is Not!* strategy. This is important for helping students to develop metacognitive awareness about the value of a given strategy to deepen their learning.

Strategy #2: *Prove it!*
(Criteria for arriving at judgements)

When I teach professionals about evaluation, I like to use the following small group exercise. I first ask each group to come up with three or four attributes that would help people to decide which is the best chocolate chip cookie. (If your participants don't eat cookies, this can be done with other foods such as different types of apples or pears.) Once they have set their criteria, I hand out three different brands of chocolate chip cookies with the branding information removed. The groups then use their criteria to rate the cookies and decide which is the best chocolate chip cookie. Inevitably, each group comes up with different sets of attributes: crunchiness, chewiness, proportion of chocolate, type of chocolate, sweetness, crumbliness, size and so on. Rarely do all groups choose the same cookie, but they are able to *Prove it!* by using their criteria.

You may want to use the cookie example or move straight to a question that piques curiosity and deepens conceptual understandings. Have students define, in advance, the attributes or criteria which they will use to make a decision or evaluate the worth of something.

***Prove it!* Example:** Invention

In order to fully engage students and activate curiosity, select questions that are big and meaningful. In the following example, we have adapted Rebecca Stonbaugh's approach from her book *Cognitive Engagement: Creating a Thinking Culture in the Classroom* (2019) by asking "What invention has most changed the way we live?"

Step 1 Generate criteria: The importance of this exercise lies in the way that the criteria are applied to assess and compare opinions. In our example, we decided to use three criteria to help us **Prove it!**: number of people in the world that have been impacted, global degree of change before and after the invention, and changes to daily activities at the individual level. What attributes do you think would be helpful for this evaluation?

Step 2 Brainstorm answers: Responses can be based on negative or positive instances, depending on the question. Here is a list of responses we came up with: wheel, airplane, nuclear weapons, smart devices (AI), spear, pen, compass, printing press, vaccines. What additional answers would you include?

Step 3 Select a few choices and apply criteria: Table 6.2 shows our responses to this question. Notice that, by design, our results will differ from those of others, thereby creating a platform for reasoned discussions around *Does it make sense?* We can use criteria to *Prove it!* in the sense of backing up an argument, but, as in the real world, there is no right answer.

Table 6.2 *Prove it!* What invention has most changed the way we live?

Invention	Criteria 1: number of people impacted	Criteria 2: degree of change	Criteria 3: changes to our lives
Invention 1: Wheel	Majority in developed and agrarian societies	Faster transportation, farming, moving things much more efficiently, pottery, water energy	Driving, biking, using a wheelbarrow, carts, toys
Invention 2: Smart devices	Most people in developed countries	Internet, replacement by robots, dealing with large databases (medicine, politics, law)	Faster data analysis, entertainment, messaging and video calls, instantaneous communications
Invention 3: Nuclear energy	Worldwide: victims of nuclear weapons, some countries have nuclear energy plants/submarines	Geopolitics related to superpowers and international treaties, ethics related to war and conflicts	Fear that our leaders or enemies will "press the button," lives and health of victims

Going through this process and comparing responses can serve as a basis for safe and respectful conversations around complex issues. Developing a muscle for thinking about something, based on criteria, can open our minds to different perspectives and allow us to discern between untested assertions and positions that pass a certain degree of scrutiny.

Strategy #3: *Grapple to Grasp*
(Retrieval practice for making meaning)

Explain to students that we are best able to grasp concepts and apply them to Critical Thinking when we have first had to grapple with learning. This requires mental effort and time. But it is worth it because, when we grapple, we deepen our understanding and store information in our long-term memories where we can access it later. Ultimately, grappling with information builds neural pathways and makes us smarter.

Grapple to Grasp Example:

Step 1 Choice of Texts: Give your students two short articles about two *different* topics: one from a source where the data and conclusions have been summarised using simplified language and minimal context; and a second article that is scientific in nature with a level of complexity that requires thinking and reasoning, yet is within their grasp (Productive Puzzling).

Step 2 Read: Simply ask your students to read the first article independently.

Step 3 Grapple: For the second article, have them work in pairs or groups to capture the key points and implications in a variety of formats, using Carefully Crafted Questions and multiple senses. Ensure that they grapple with the material, manipulate the information and make it their own by understanding, explaining and recording it in their own ways.

Step 4 Pop Quiz: A week later, give them a pop quiz on each article (not for a grade) and have students identify what they do and don't know.

Step 5 Reflection: Use these results to demonstrate that, when we simply read information, we are being passive and we are more likely to forget the material. When we need to access the materials and apply it for thinking critically, it's gone. On the other hand, by doing the work to dig deep to uncover the meaning of the data and draw conclusions, we are grappling with the information, understanding it further, remembering the ideas and preparing our brains to think critically about the concepts. If students want to grasp and apply concepts in the long term, they have to grapple with the material.

When retrieval practice is used to more thoroughly understand what you are learning, it becomes an executive function strategy and not simply a form of assessment (Agarwal et al. 2017). To cultivate joy in learning, students need countless experiences with retrieving information and using it to ask *Does it make sense?* without any grade attached. If this becomes a habit, they are more likely to direct their own learning and to question authority. The purpose of this activity is to give students the opportunity to experience what happens when we spend focused mental effort figuring something out and really 'get it'.

Critical Thinking in action: a social justice example from grade 1

Bret Turner is a former first grade teacher in Oakland, California. Conversations about power and privilege had been ongoing in his class as they relate to a variety of topics. While studying homelessness, his six year old students discovered that a disproportionate number of homeless people in their county were black. Rather than simply leave this discovery as a fact, Mr Turner recognised this as an opportunity to explore the question *Does this make sense?* He began this discussion by making his thinking visible. He shared that he was questioning why half of the homeless people in their county were black because it didn't make sense or seem fair to him. Mr Turner opened up the discussion to his students with the questions, "What do we know about what causes homelessness?" and "What causes people to be pushed down rather than lifted up?" These types of knowledge based questions help students to clarify the facts that provide the basis for developing criteria to assess if something makes sense or not. His students identified such things as unemployment and racism as contributing factors. What began as an observation about homelessness in their county, turned into a lesson about how to think critically about inequity and structural racism. For example, one student made the connection between people being denied jobs and 'the color of their skin'. With this type of ongoing discussion, Mr Turner is providing a framework for how to think about and grapple with important issues that impact people's lives, even in the youngest of students.

(Schwartz 2019)

Review this example and think about the conditions required for Productive Puzzling. What does Mr Turner do to support Productive Puzzling? Consider:

- trusting relationships (condition 1);
- challenge balanced with solutions that are within reach (conditions 2 and 3);
- multiple strategies (condition 4); and
- reflection (condition 5).

Independent reflection, individual autonomy and reasoning skills all flow from using explicit strategies for thinking critically. (To track progress in your

Productive Puzzling in action

Table 6.3 Flexible Learning Activation Checklist (FLAC): <u>C</u>ritical Thinking

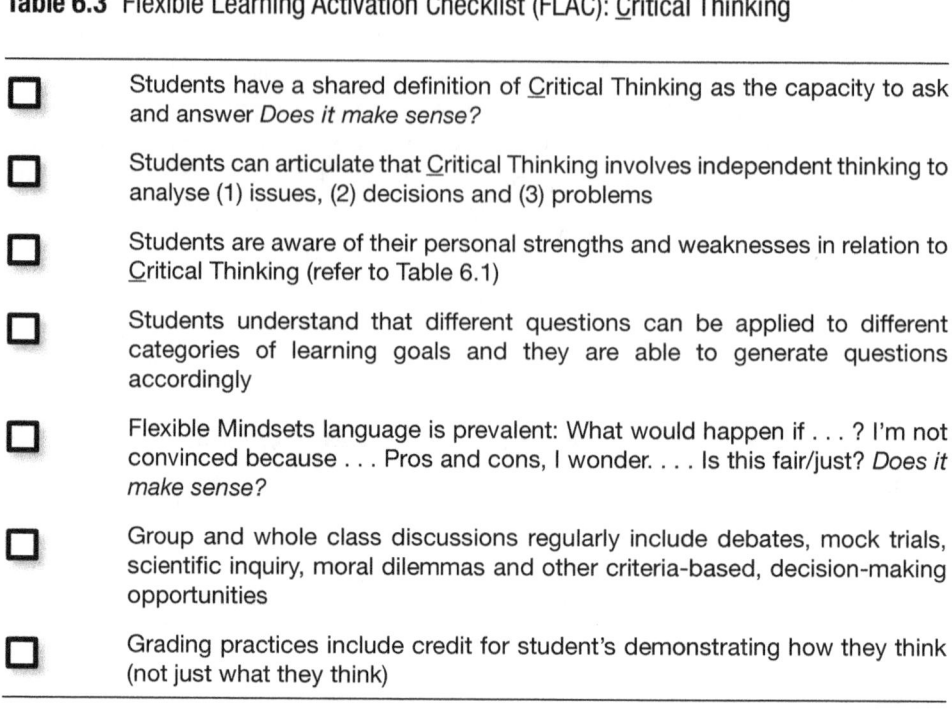

☐	Students have a shared definition of <u>C</u>ritical Thinking as the capacity to ask and answer *Does it make sense?*
☐	Students can articulate that <u>C</u>ritical Thinking involves independent thinking to analyse (1) issues, (2) decisions and (3) problems
☐	Students are aware of their personal strengths and weaknesses in relation to <u>C</u>ritical Thinking (refer to Table 6.1)
☐	Students understand that different questions can be applied to different categories of learning goals and they are able to generate questions accordingly
☐	Flexible Mindsets language is prevalent: What would happen if . . . ? I'm not convinced because . . . Pros and cons, I wonder. . . . Is this fair/just? *Does it make sense?*
☐	Group and whole class discussions regularly include debates, mock trials, scientific inquiry, moral dilemmas and other criteria-based, decision-making opportunities
☐	Grading practices include credit for student's demonstrating how they think (not just what they think)

classroom, you can use some of the items in Table 6.3). Ultimately, <u>C</u>ritical Thinking is the antidote to oppressive systems and authoritarian regimes. Ultimately, we need learners who are committed to developing and applying thinking capacities as the first step in creating a more equitable world and responding to the unexpected.

"Doubt is the beginning, not the end of wisdom."

(George Iles)

Productive Puzzling and <u>C</u>ritical Thinking: retrieval practice

For the first three rows in Table 6.4, you may wish to use retrieval practice to help you grapple with your conceptions about <u>C</u>ritical Thinking. Cover up the right hand column and record your responses. Once you have completed your responses, unveil the right hand column and use the information from this chapter to expand your ideas.

Table 6.4 Productive Puzzling and Critical Thinking: retrieval practice

QUESTION	WHAT DO YOU REMEMBER?
What is Critical Thinking?	The capacity to ask and answer the question: *Does it make sense?*
What is the key tool for Critical Thinking?	Developing and applying criteria
What strategies can we use to build Critical Thinking capacities? Create specific content-based examples of these strategies that you can use with your students.	1 *Is! Is Not!* 2 *Prove it!* 3 *Grapple to Grasp* 4 ...
Using the Flexible Mindsets framework, what will you do right away to help students further develop Critical Thinking capacities?	
What single practice will you shift to encourage students to see themselves as capable and competent as critical thinkers who analyse issues, decisions and problems? (words we use to describe ourselves and our work, group discussions, grading, etc.)	
How will you get your students to: ■ identify a practice in their school/community/world that is unjust? ■ encourage them to think critically about the contributing factors? ■ use Critical Thinking strategies to take action?	

References

Agarwal, P., Finley, J., Rose, N., & Roediger, H. (2017). Benefits from retrieval practice are greater for students with lower working memory capacity. *Memory.* **25**, 764–771.

Brown, P., Roediger, H., & McDaniel, M. (2014). *Make it stick: The science of successful learning.* Cambridge, MA: The Belknap Press of Harvard University Press.

Cooper, N. (2018). What effect do questions have on our brain? [online]. *Medium.com.* 15 March 2018. [Viewed 3 March 2020]. Available from: https://medium.com/@mr.neilcooper/what-effect-do-questions-have-on-our-brain-329c37d69948

Hoffeld, D. (2017). Want to know what your brain does when it hears a question? [online]. 21 February 2017. [Viewed 17 July 2020]. Available from: www.fastcompany.com/3068341/want-to-know-what-your-brain-does-when-it-hears-a-question

Medina, J. (2008). *Brain rules: 12 principles for surviving and thriving at work, home, and school.* Seattle, WA: Pear Press.

Schwartz, K. (2019). Teaching 6-year-olds about privilege and power [online]. *KQED.* 17 September 2019. [Viewed 15 March 2020]. Available from: www.kqed.org/mindshift/54150/teaching-6-year-olds-about-privilege-and-power

Stonbaugh, R. (2019). *Cognitive engagement: Creating a thinking culture in the classroom.* Bloomington, IN: Solution Tree Press.

Wineburg, S., Breakstone, J., Ziv, N., & Smith, M. (2020). *Educating for misunderstanding: How approaches to teaching digital literacy make students susceptible to scammers, rogues, bad actors, and hate mongers* (Working Paper A-21322). Stanford History Education Group. Available from: https://purl.stanford.edu/mf412bt5333

CHAPTER

Complex Problem-Solving
What else can we try?

Imagine you are a geoengineer. Wait! What's a geoengineer? Geoengineering is a field that is developing rapidly in response to the climate change crisis. Geoengineers deliberately manipulate the Earth's climate (Pearce 2019). Their efforts are controversial and raise ethical questions around carbon emissions. The field is also under scrutiny due to inherent challenges in predicting the potential negative effects of geoengineered solutions. Geoengineering cannot rely on traditional scientific inquiry because their proposals are very costly and we can't reverse the effects of our actions if it is determined that they are too harmful (Yale E360 2019). Some cutting edge proposals for reducing the impact of climate change include:

- installation of orbital mirrors in the atmosphere to reflect sunlight back into space;
- fertilisation of oceans using iron that causes large blooms of algae or phytoplankton which absorb CO_2 and take it with them to the floor of the ocean when they die; and
- designing artificial trees: tree-like machines that 'scrub' the air clean of pollution.
(Aouf 2018)

Picture yourself as a member of a geoengineering team. You have been presented with the complex problem of reducing the effects of global warming. Select one of these three ideas and consider whether or not it is an effective solution. What are the key underlying causes of global warming? What potential harms may result from these solutions? Do the consequences of geoengineering projects such as these outweigh the benefits of reducing the effects of carbon emissions? *What else can we try?*

As we noted in the preface to this book, the problems that today's young people will face are more complex and existential than we could have imagined a few decades ago. Solutions are messy. These real-world problems can serve as a key motivator for young people, providing the impetus to teach Complex Problem-Solving through Productive Puzzling.

We have the power and the responsibility to prepare learners to use multifaceted strategies to define, analyse and solve problems. Educators are committed to presenting students with authentic problems and teaching ways to solve them. However, many curricula place greater priority on content, with problem-solving often relegated to a lesser role. There is minimal transfer from academic learning to meaningful problems encountered in the lives of our students. Some of these problems may be directly school related such as unfamiliar math word problems, collaborative projects or novel research assignments. However, meaningful problems are the unexpected logistical and interpersonal challenges we experience both in and outside of school. There are real consequences that individuals experience daily from problems such as designing work for machines, upskilling for a new job, facing moral dilemmas, struggling with personal debt, or starting, running and managing change for a business. These are the types of problems that we must prepare learners to puzzle through and solve (see Figure 7.1).

> In this chapter, we will:
>
> 1 share the Flexible Mindsets definition of Complex Problem-Solving;
> 2 describe what happens in the brain when we solve problems;
> 3 provide three strategies to help students ask and answer: *What else can we try?*;
> 4 share an example of an eight year old engaged in Complex Problem-Solving; and
> 5 present items from the Flexible Learning Activation Checklist (FLAC) that educators can use to track progress in designing environments that promote Complex Problem-Solving.

Figure 7.1 Complex Problem-Solving: *What else can we try?*

Flexible Mindsets definition of Complex Problem-Solving

Complex Problem-Solving is the capacity for unravelling an ambiguous puzzle by tackling obstacles and thinking through multiple strategies to find one or more solution(s).

Our main departure from common definitions of problem-solving lies in our conceptualisations about what makes a problem a problem. To engage learners in Productive Puzzling, we must balance challenge with attainable solutions and a precise degree of complexity. Provocations allow and encourage children to experience the world for themselves through open-ended activities without being overtly guided by a teacher or parent. The idea behind provocations is to encourage children to think independently by encouraging their interests and the exploration of those interests. You cannot have a provocation without spurring learners to ask *What else can we try?* To illustrate what constitutes a problem, we explore two examples and counterexamples:

1. Mathematics is a relatively straightforward area for considering the nature of a problem. In early elementary school, students are assigned word problems, starting with something as simple as:

   Ashleigh has 3 cookies and Mateo has 2. How many cookies do they have altogether? Is this a problem? If a child is encountering this structure for the first time and is required to ponder before making a response, then it is a problem or puzzle. As soon as the student has become familiar with this format and can complete a set of similar items fluently, it is no longer a problem.

2. Similarly, in literature, the protagonist usually encounters one or more problems or ethical dilemmas that are not easily solved. When students are initially asked to predict how a character will solve a problem, they have to analyse the character's goal and circumstances and then consider possible solutions. However, genres such as traditional folk tales often follow a script that can become foreseeable. As a student's responses become more automatic, they are no longer puzzling.

Some experts make the distinction between routine standard problems and non-routine or nonstandard problems (Abdullah et al. 2014). We make a similar distinction between practice and puzzling. Hence our use of the term Complex Problem-Solving to differentiate between routines and Productive Puzzling.

Our definition of a complex problem (puzzle) is further elucidated in Table 7.1.

Complex problems are meaty and messy and often derive from provocations. Effective provocations are designed to evoke curiosity and interest and serve as the jumping off points for learners to investigate and think independently. They can be set up using any open-ended materials, including novel objects and things found in nature. The aim is to stimulate thoughts, discussion and questions and to expand ideas. Provocations have no wrong outcomes and feed the imagination.

Table 7.1 Flexible Mindsets criteria for complex problems

A complex problem is not . . .	A complex problem is . . .
■ Boring	■ Engaging
■ Familiar	■ Novel
■ Decontextualised	■ Authentic (embedded in the real world)
■ Passive	■ Emotionally evocative due to risk involved and potential consequences
■ Straightforward	■ Perplexing or messy
■ Unidimensional	■ Multifaceted (derived from multiple causes)
■ Solved using only one strategy (approach)	■ Approachable from different perspectives (using different strategies)
■ Answered with one "right" solution	■ Designed for multiple and often inexact responses (ideally)

Ultimately, through provocations, students can experience the world for themselves and explore freely (The Compass School 2017).

Complex problems involve trial and error, testing theories, cause and effect thinking and learning from mistakes. They are not solved quickly. If you give students word problems and they complete all items fluently and accurately, that is practice, not puzzling. Today, hundreds of mathematical problems remain unsolved, many of which were proposed over a century ago!

Productive Puzzling can be deepened by targeting the development of the characteristics associated with successful problem-solving. In Flexible Mindsets, we prioritise the roles of generating, transferring and applying multiple strategies through Productive Puzzling to ask the question *What else can we try?* The ongoing engagement of constructive problem-solvers leads them to:

- enjoy sinking their teeth into a good challenge;
- value the discomfort that comes with provocation;
- think strategically and evaluate solutions;
- share and discuss strategies;
- reflect on and explain their learning (Today I learned . . . , I'm still not sure about . . . , I think the answer is _____ because . . .);
- collaborate and be open to different ideas and ways of thinking;
- tolerate confusion and partial understanding;
- generate multiple strategies for tackling problems;
- take into account ethics, social justice and the human element;
- accept failure as a valuable step in learning; and
- take breaks from focused thought to engage in diffuse thinking.

What happens in the brain when we solve complex problems?

We've all experienced the elation that accompanies a true 'Aha!' moment. It's a perfect combination of astonishment and deep satisfaction that drives us to seek more of these moments (Sprugnoli et al. 2017). Leveraging the satisfaction derived from discovering a solution is key when we are faced with complex problems. Wouldn't it be great if there was a way to channel this drive for 'Aha!' moments into everyday learning? It turns out that, with a bit of knowledge about what happens in the brain when we problem solve, we can structure learning environments that increase the likelihood of 'Aha!' moments.

Problem-solving generally falls into three categories: analytical problem-solving, memory retrieval and insight. Analytical problem-solving is deliberate and we are at least somewhat aware of what we are doing because we follow steps and can explain how we arrived at a solution. Problem-solving that involves memory retrieval requires a simple retrieval of knowledge that already exists and applying that to a current problem. Insight problem-solving on the other hand, consists of an 'Aha!' moment that is unexpected and cannot be explained by a sequential solution process. Another key component of insight problem-solving is a sense of being stuck before arriving at a solution. This type of problem-solving is deeply embedded in the brain's architecture and has kept humans alive for so long by linking a solution to a brief, but deep feeling of euphoria. The feelings that occur at the moment of insight are caused by a flood of the neurochemical dopamine into a part of the brain called the nucleus accumbens. The nucleus accumbens is active throughout the process of problem-solving, but particularly so at the moment of insight. This part of the brain, in the basal forebrain, is part of the dopamine network that is triggered when we receive a reward. So, in essence, the brain lights up when we solve a tricky problem (Sprugnoli et al. 2017).

Metacognition applied to Complex Problem-Solving

Metacognitive Insights

As with any meaningful learning, Complex Problem-Solving is anchored in self-reflection. Students must develop an awareness of their own strengths and weaknesses, multiple viewpoints and the strategies we use to solve problems.

Before they can learn problem-solving strategies, learners must first be able to recognise when something is not right. This Metacognitive Insight is critical for identifying that there is a problem. We know in our gut when there is a problem, even if we can't put it into words. We might feel uncomfortable, concerned, disappointed or confused because we have encountered an incongruity that we have not yet named. These signals should not be ignored and are the first step in identifying and solving problems.

Start by facilitating a process for a common definition of the term problem using brainstorming and consensus building. Have students explore questions such as "How do we know when there is a problem? What examples can we come up with where there is a clear difference between what is and what should be, what is just and what is unjust? When presented with a puzzle (problem), where do we start? What are some problem-solving strategies that we already know and/or use? What are the benefits of mistakes and struggling as we try to solve complex problems? *What else can we try?*" Then encourage students to reflect on their own strengths and weaknesses in terms of identifying and solving problems. You may wish to use a simple format such as the one presented in Table 7.2 which presents sample items from the Metacognitive Insights Survey (MIS) as part of our Flexible Learning Environmental Scan (FLES) (see also Appendix B).

Table 7.2 Metacognitive Insights Survey (MIS): Complex Problem-Solving

Complex Problem-Solving item	Yes	Sort of	Not Yet
I view challenges as opportunities to grow			
I notice when I am confused or don't fully understand something and use that to fuel my curiosity			
I am able to generate multiple solutions to a problem			
I am aware of the strategies I'm using and can talk about them with others			
I respect the perspectives of others when attempting to solve problems			
When I try to solve problems, my intent is to find solutions that are fair, just and ethical			
I believe that failure is necessary in order to learn			

Multiple perspectives

Complex Problem-Solving, by definition, requires learners to conceptualise issues from multiple perspectives. If the first strategy you use works right away, you are not engaged in Productive Puzzling. Multiple perspectives are required for solving puzzles by:

1. Taking into account all the *different factors* that define a problem: This is an area that is already addressed in many educational settings. However, direct instruction, modelling and practice will prepare learners for transferring problem analysis into the real-world context. If you have completed a school day without engaging students in examining multiple causes of and influences on a problem, then prioritise this for the next available opportunity.
2. Viewing problems from *different perspectives*: Without flexible thinking, it is impossible to understand that a problem can be interpreted in different ways. Many learners take other perspectives naturally, but in the classroom context, it is important to provide direct instruction. We can start with multiple meaning words and sentences. Humour can be used to illustrate that there can be different ways to interpret something such as *The last time I stole a calendar, I got 12 months*. Key learning takes place as you provide models and practice and constantly point out differences in how problems can be seen. Learning deepens when we use language such as:

> "You think of it like this and I see it this way. Some people view this puzzle as similar to ___. How else can we look at this?"

> "Imagine a conversation between J. Robert Oppenheimer and James Baldwin about using violence to end violence. What might each of them say about the nature of the problem and how to solve it?"

Educators sometimes feel that there is not enough time to explore problems in enough depth. Yet, if we believe in equity and in the survival of our planet, we cannot afford to stay on our current path. It is up to us to teach strategies and ensure that representation and counternarratives are priorities. Dr Ainissa Ramirez is a former associate professor of Mechanical Engineering and Materials Science at

Yale University (2012). She has become a champion for making science fun for all learners. Her outlook on science embodies the tenets of Flexible Mindsets:

> Students need to explore and discover in science. This is how you innovate; you fail your way to the answer. Scientists fail all the time; we just brand it differently: we call it data.

Flexible Mindset strategies for Complex Problem-Solving

The strategies presented in this section are designed to help students find ways to answer the question *What else can we try?*

Strategy #1: *Mix Master* Interleaving so I can solve problems flexibly
Strategy #2: *Fork in the Road* Shifting strategies when I'm stuck
Strategy #3: *Mind Reminder* Analogical thinking and retrieval practice

Strategy #1: *Mix Master*
(Interleaving so I can solve problems flexibly)

Interleaving refers to the strategy of switching between different types of problems (Rohrer 2012). It helps us recognise patterns, distinguish concepts and apply strategies. When we are interleaving we are making connections for long-term learning and retention. Mixing up problems, or interleaving, is more effective than blocked or massed practice (focusing on a single topic or subject) because it helps our brain to categorise, problem solve and transfer information. When using the strategy of interleaving, students can't rely on the rote responses that are stored in short-term memory in a rote structure. Their brains will need to continually retrieve information because each idea is different from the last. To effectively employ the strategy of interleaving, students need to mix multiple subjects or topics while they study.

Step 1 What is interleaving?: Give students a simple definition of interleaving such as 'moving back and forth between concepts and mixing up the order'. Help students understand the value of switching between different types of problems when they learn. Explain that when we mix things up, our struggle helps us to understand concepts on a deeper level and to retrieve information more easily and for longer periods of time.

Step 2 Direct practice: Teach students to study for tests by switching between different types of questions that focus on different types of problems or concepts. Encourage them to circle back to material and make sure they do it in a different order. This forces the brain to be flexible. Explain that each time you study a problem or concept, you should make sure you understand something before switching to another topic or subject. We don't want students to use interleaving as an excuse when they are stuck, bored or the material is too difficult. Rather than thinking "This problem just got really hard, I don't know what to do, I'm going to switch to the next section," have students persist instead (including asking for help) until they achieve a *sense of accomplishment*. Then switch.

Strategy #2: *Fork in the Road*
(Shifting strategies when I'm stuck)

Use this when a strategy is not working or when we don't have everything available to easily solve a puzzle. When something is blocking our way, it is often easy to become discouraged. Practising Flexible Mindsets habits frees us to use a 'Fork in the Road' approach by:

- clarifying our goal;
- recognising when we are stuck;
- identifying the obstacles to reaching our goal;
- examining what we have already tried; and
- using that knowledge to modify or switch to another strategy.

This can be achieved through play and for fun. The *Fork in the Road* strategy can be applied to all stages of development and across all topics.

Step 1 Explain the goal: Let students know that the question *What else can we try?* needs to become a habit we use even when you're not stuck. By generating more than one strategy for solving a problem, we are able to consider problems at a deeper level and then choose which road to follow, which direction to take.

Step 2 Brainstorm practice: Here are a few examples you could adapt and use with your students (Table 7.3):

Have a discussion about this type of activity. Just by going through this process, learners should come away with a strategy that helps them to clarify goals and explain the nature of a problem to others. In essence, you are leading them to discover that:

Goal + Obstacle = Puzzle (Complex Problem)

Table 7.3 'Fork in the Road' strategy for Complex Problem-Solving

Goal	Obstacle(s)	What has been tried?	What else can we try?
Fabiella's friend keeps teasing Anya, a girl at their school – Fabbi would like her to stop	Fabiella doesn't want her friend to get mad at her	trying to steer her friend away from Anya; trying to console Anya	■ "I notice you said something that made Anya sad. How do you feel about Anya?"; ■ ask the school counsellor for help.
Seamus wants to start his own business selling his artwork	He doesn't know where to start	Googled 'start a business' (overwhelmed by too much stuff)	■ talk to entrepreneurs who have started businesses; ■ use resources for small business that offer training.
Virtual learning is becoming the main way to learn in some schools	Some students don't have a laptop or access to the internet	A donor gave 200 laptops to a school but the school didn't have the tech support to set them up	■ ask IT professionals to donate time; ■ get free internet subscriptions for all the homes; ■ set up a buddy system where students can go to a friend's house to do schoolwork/homework.

Step 3 Extend the discussion: Ask students to examine similarities and differences between the solutions that they have generated. Class discussions often lead to the conclusion that the *Fork in the Road* strategy forces us to recognise there is a puzzle with multiple solutions and then to persist, identify obstacles, seek work arounds, work with others, substitute an element of the puzzle or modify the goal.

Step 4 Make it important: As long as we continue to reinforce the practices that overvalue rote learning, students will apply little effort to build the capacity for solving complex problems. To help them shift to a more balanced set of priorities, we need to move beyond exposure and feedback. Grading systems offer a ready opportunity to have students share the process of considering multiple strategies and outcomes.

Strategy #3: *Mind Reminder*
(Analogical thinking and retrieval practice)

An analogy is a way to compare two or more ideas that share significant features. Analogies are typically used for the purpose of explanation or clarification. Analogical reasoning can afford students a distinct advantage for transferring learning from one context to another, provided that they receive explicit instruction in content areas related to science, literacy and mathematics. We need to directly teach learners how to recognise the similarity of relational structure between a known solved problem and a novel problem. Instructional approaches may include: scaffolding opportunities to make comparisons between newly learned concepts and previously learned ones, presenting source and target analogies simultaneously with additional cues (such as gestures), and highlighting similarities and differences between sources and targets.

Mind Reminder Example: Understanding the functions of cell parts (grade 6 science)

Step 1 What is an analogy?: Ensure that students are familiar with a simple definition of an analogy such as 'a comparison of two things to show their similarities'. A few simple examples can be introduced such as *If a bird flies in the sky, then a fish swims in the sea* or *We must come out of our comfort zone like a butterfly emerges from its cocoon.*

Step 2 What does this remind me of?: Help your students to brainstorm about how this problem is similar to something they have solved before. Initially, you will need to guide and suggest ideas until students become more comfortable with the process. In this example, students are taught to create the analogy of a house to represent the parts of a human cell where:

- the cell membrane can be conceptualised as a door;
- the nucleus, as the centre of the cell, may be seen as the family room;
- the mitochondria convert nutrients into energy and can be compared to a fire or furnace;
- the lysosomes remove waste and can be likened to garbage cans or compost heaps; and
- vacuoles store nutrients and would be analogous to storage closets.

Step 3 How do we see this?: Have students work in small groups to represent the analogous elements in creative ways (drawing, mindmap, video clip, poem).

Step 3 Pop Quiz: A week later, give them a pop quiz (not for a grade) on the topic and have students identify what they do and don't know.

Note that this differs fundamentally from a mnemonic to help learners memorise rote material. Creating the analogy requires deeper understanding of the concepts. You cannot retrieve the cell part without making the analogy to its function. This degree of puzzling is critical for preparing students to solve novel problems using analogies.

Once your students have worked through some examples with you, they will be ready to start retrieving their existing knowledge and connecting it to new conceptual problems at a basic level. This is complex and requires mental effort, so continued modelling and practice are critical for developing this capacity.

Complex Problem-Solving in the moment: an energy solution from an eight-year-old

> An eight year old girl named Xóchitl Guadalupe Cruz from Chiapas, Mexico has invented a solar powered water heater out of recycled materials that will bring warm water to those who don't have easy access. The impact her invention could have on others around the world is immense and this has inspired the National Autonomous University of Mexico's Institute of Nuclear Sciences to recognise her. Cruz's device was inspired by the desire to reduce deforestation and pollution by replacing the need to cut logs for heating water, which is the primary method used to heat water where she lives. Cruz furthers her commitment to environmentally sound practices by utilising recycled materials to build her device. Her solar powered invention has the potential to improve the quality of life for millions around the world who still rely on wood as the primary source of fuel for heating water.
>
> (Padgett 2019)

Consider the problem-solving of Xóchitl and the degree to which she was engaged in Productive Puzzling:

- What factors may have contributed to Xóchitl's comfort level for risk-taking? (condition 1).
- Was this problem challenging for Xóchitl? Were solutions within reach? (conditions 2 and 3).
- How do you think this problem required Xóchitl to consider multiple strategies and use trial and error? (condition 4).
- What evidence is there that Xóchitl engaged in reflection about her proposed solution and other potential solutions? (condition 5).

If we are to prepare students for the challenges of today and tomorrow, we must lead an ongoing, explicit and cyclical campaign to empower them to solve complex problems and learn HOW to learn. (Please refer to Table 7.4 for ways to track progress in your classroom). Uncertain times demand problem-solvers who understand that the world is messy, can listen to the perspectives of others and use both ethical principles and cognitive strategies to make the world a better place.

Table 7.4 Flexible Learning Activation Checklist (FLAC): Complex Problem-Solving

☐	Students have a shared definition of Complex Problem-Solving as the capacity to ask and answer *What else can we try?*
☐	Students have a shared understanding of the nature of a complex problem (puzzle)
☐	Students can articulate that Complex Problem-Solving involves: (1) puzzles with more than one answer; (2) tackling obstacles; (3) multiple perspectives; and (4) thinking through or trying out multiple strategies
☐	Students are aware of their personal strengths and weaknesses in relation to Complex Problem-Solving (refer to Table 7.2)
☐	Work displayed/student portfolios include examples of strategies attempted that didn't work; more than one strategy to use; and more than one solution to a problem
☐	Flexible Mindsets language is prevalent: goal, strategy, other perspectives, persevere, one answer could be . . . because . . ., ethical considerations, *What else can we try?*
☐	Small group and whole class discussions regularly include sharing of strategies, discussions of ethical considerations and examples of learning from mistakes
☐	Grading practices include credit for students' self-reflections about strategies for problem-solving
☐	Particular emphasis and credit is given to solutions that are sourced in empathy, reflect outside-of-the-box thinking and put forward counternarratives

Productive Puzzling for Complex Problem-Solving: retrieval practice

As you ponder about this chapter, you may wish to use retrieval practice by covering the right-hand column in the first three rows of Table 7.5 and seeing what you know in regards to the left-hand column. Remember, if you struggle then you are puzzling productively!

Table 7.5 Productive Puzzling and Complex Problem-Solving: retrieval practice

QUESTION	WHAT DO YOU REMEMBER?
What is Complex Problem-Solving?	The ability to ask and answer the question: What else could we try?
What is the key tool for Complex Problem-Solving?	Shifting perspectives

Table 7.5 (Continued)

QUESTION	WHAT DO YOU REMEMBER?
What strategies can we teach students to grow their Complex Problem-Solving capacities? Create specific content-based examples of these strategies that you can use with your students.	1 *Mind Reminder* 2 *Mix Master* 3 *Fork in the Road* 4 . . .
What single practice will you shift to encourage students to see themselves as capable and competent at solving problems, tackling obstacles and seeing things from different perspectives? (words we use to describe ourselves and our work, group discussions, grading, etc.)	
How will you get your students to: ■ identify a problem that is meaningful? ■ brainstorm potential solutions? ■ evaluate strategies through the lens of equity?	

References

Abdullah, A. H., Ibrahim, N., Surif, J., Ali, M., & Hamzah, M. (2014). Non-routine mathematical problems among in-service and pre-service mathematics teachers [online]. *IEEE International Conference on Teaching, Assessment and Learning for Engineering*. 19 March 2015. [Viewed 13 January 2019]. Available from: doi: 10.1109/TALE.2014.7062620

Aouf, R. (2018). Five geoengineering solutions proposed to fight climate change [online]. *de zeen*. 18 October 2018. [Viewed 15 April 2020]. Available at: www.dezeen.com/2018/10/18/five-geoengineering-solutions-climate-change-un-ipcc-technology/

The Compass School. (2017). What is a provocation? Encouraging your child's interests [online]. *The Compass School*. 16 August 2017. [Viewed 9 June 2020]. Available from: www.thecompassschool.com/blog/what-is-provocation/

Padgett, T. (2019). Meet Mexico's new famous inventor. She'll finish third grade this year [online]. *WLRN The Takeaway*. 7 March 2019. [Viewed 17 July 2020]. Available from: www.wlrn.org/news/2019-03-07/meet-mexicos-new-famous-inventor-shell-finish-third-grade-this-year

Pearce, F. (2019). Geoengineer the planet? More scientists now say it must be an option [online]. *Yale E360*. 29 May 2019 [Viewed 24 May 2020]. Available from: https://e360.yale.edu/features/geoengineer-the-planet-more-scientists-now-say-it-must-be-an-option

Ramirez, A. (2012). Save our Science Sputnik Moment for STEM education [online]. *TEDBlog*. 2 March 2012. [Viewed 1 April 2020]. Available from: https://blog.ted.com/a-sputnik-moment-for-stem-education-ainissa-ramirez-at-ted2012/

Rohrer, D. (2012). Interleaving helps students distinguish among similar concepts. *Educational Psychology Review*. **24**, 355–367.

Sprugnoli, G., Rossi, S., Emmendorfer, A., Rossi, A., Liew, S.-L., Tatti, E., di Lorenzo, G., Pascual-Leone, A., & Santarnecchi, E. (2017). Neural correlates of Eureka moment. *Intelligence*. **62**, 99–118.

CHAPTER

Creativity
What are the possibilities?

Never before has there been such emphasis on the role of Creativity. Businesses know that their survival depends on the ongoing flow of ideas for new services and products. Many of them encourage employees to allocate 20% of their work time to thinking creatively and exploring new ideas. At a global level, Creativity has been cited as the most important quality to meet the challenges of complexity and the uncertainty of our times (IBM 2010).

On an individual level, the advent of artificial intelligence has fundamentally changed the workforce. Automation has replaced many jobs that used to depend on rote tasks. Upskilling, on its own, does not offer us a layer of protection against becoming irrelevant and possibly unemployable. Creativity is increasingly recognised as a pathway to future achievements for employees, entrepreneurs and freelancers.

In a recent State of Create global survey, 76% of respondents viewed unlocking creative potential as essential for economic growth. In contrast, only 31% of participants felt they were living up to their creative potential. Furthermore, 65% agreed that their Creativity is being *stifled* by the education system (Adobe 2016). This illustrates the gap between the desire to have creative ideas and our struggles to understand the nature of Creativity: people want to be more creative, but don't know how to unlock their potential.

Everyone has creative capacities. We all have imaginative ideas that, when mingled with those of others, allow Creativity to flourish. When children enter school, their minds are full of imagination and play-based learning supports Creativity. As they progress through school, kids become more and more afraid to share their ideas. This happens in microsteps over time as curricular demands and fixed mentalities deter the exploration of ideas and out-of-the-box thinking. Sir Ken Robinson (2017), a thought leader on Creativity and innovation, describes imagination as lying at the root of Creativity where we are able to bring to mind things that are not immediately present, where we can visit the past and envision possible futures. Sir Ken's concerns about the decline of Creativity and the phenomenon through which it disappears are widely known. His critiques echo those that have been expressed for decades. For example, a longitudinal study used a Creativity test that was devised for selecting NASA scientists (Land 2020). The proportion of people scoring at the genius level fell from 98% at five years old to 30% at ten years old and 12% at age 15. Despite these seemingly grim statistics, the underlying capacity for Creativity is not lost. We can always become engaged in exploring *What are the possibilities?* (See Figure 8.1.)

These challenges present opportunities that are both compelling and exciting. Educators have always shaped the minds of the future. Now, more than ever, we will need resourceful ideas to stimulate Creativity. This is our moment to envision the future, its possibilities and our collective hopes. Imagination, innovation and inventiveness will determine that future.

Imagination is more important than knowledge. For knowledge is limited to all we now know and understand, while imagination embraces the entire world and all there ever will be to know and understand.

(Albert Einstein)

In this chapter, we will:

1. present the Flexible Mindsets definition of Creativity;
2. describe what happens in the brain when we imagine;
3. provide ideas for teaching strategies to ask and answer: *What are the possibilities?*;
4. share an example of a teenager's inventiveness; and
5. present items from the Flexible Learning Activation Checklist (FLAC) educators can use to track progress towards an environment where Creativity can flourish.

Figure 8.1 Creativity: *What are the possibilities?*

Flexible Mindsets definition of Creativity

In the Flexible Mindsets framework, *Creativity is the synergy of thoughts to generate ideas that are imaginative, divergent and worthwhile*. This is largely influenced by Kaufman and Sternberg, whose description of creative ideas includes novelty, innovativeness and relevance (2010).

Creativity is a capacity that is often misunderstood. Many people associate Creativity with the giants of originality such as Leonardo da Vinci, Maya Angelou, Henry Ford, Bob Marley, Georgia O'Keeffe, Sir Richard Branson, Maya Lin or Joni Mitchell. Traditional perspectives see Creativity as something fanciful, rather than essential. In education, Creativity is central in early childhood and in working with 'gifted' children, but does not play a central role in general education (Feldman & Benjamin 2006). However, experts have warned for decades that we are eliminating fantastical thinking from children in the early grades, resulting in 'impoverished imaginations' (Torrance 1959). More recently, researchers in the field of Creativity have made the distinction between examples of rare creative expression and those creative experiences and expressions that are accessible to everyone (Kozbelt, Beghetto & Runco 2010; Richards 2007). This is similar to the notion of 'schoolhouse giftedness' as conceptualised by Renzulli (Renzulli & Reis 2018). In the Flexible Mindsets model, all learners have the capacity for imagination, inventiveness and innovation. Creativity is not the exclusive domain of those who are gifted with some kind of mystical talent. It is about possibilities.

Creativity researcher Edward Clapp, in his book *Participatory Creativity*, proposes moving away from attaching Creativity to a person and reframing Creativity as the biography of an idea (2017). When conceived in this way, Creativity becomes much more expansive and accessible by a variety of people in various different contexts. Collaborative Creativity acknowledges the impact of extrapersonal and sociocultural influence and the necessary balance between constraints on behaviour and freedom for novelty (Sawyer 2006). Neuroscientist David Eagleman and composer Anthony Brandt (2017) describe Creativity as a conversation between personal impulse and the community that sees it. The true value of Creativity lies in its potential to see the world around us and imagine collective possibilities.

In the Flexible Mindsets model, Creativity is participatory and interactive. It is a shared generative process. Creativity frees the mind in a way that enables people to absorb knowledge more easily and to use alternative ways of thinking that are nonlinear and open ended. Creativity connects us with our passions, gives us a voice without the limitation of words and enables us to be active participants in a process. Because our approach to Creativity inherently requires shared ideas, it helps us to build intercultural connections, broaden our perspectives and develop empathy through expanding our worldview. Creativity fosters resilience and is characterised by an eagerness to tackle challenges and embrace failures. It is the foundation for imagination, innovation and invention. The shared creative process is stimulating, motivating, fun, joyful, surprising, passionate, future thinking and hopeful.

People who continuously engage in developing creative ideas:

- get messy and welcome failure;
- come together with a common goal;
- chain ideas together in a variety of directions;
- have many associations for a concept and move fluently from obvious associations to remote ones;
- balance divergent and convergent thinking to produce ideas that are both original and effective;
- explore, discover and communicate possibilities;
- go beyond themselves to consider a larger worldview;
- embrace challenges and take risks;
- connect reflection with action; and
- are committed to equity and social justice.

What happens in the brain when we imagine?

As science has advanced newer methods for brain imaging, researchers have been able to more clearly identify regions in the brain associated with Creativity. Most notable is the discovery that Creativity is connected to flexibility in activating and deactivating brain networks (Kaufman & Gregoire 2015). The executive attention network needs to be activated to gather and absorb information and integrate it with different sensory systems. Activation also occurs in the imagination network responsible for allowing us to do things we have never tried before. In order for Creativity to really thrive, the brain networks associated with processing visual stimuli need to be deactivated at least for a moment. John Kounios, brain sciences professor at Drexel University, calls this a 'brain blink' (Kounios & Beeman 2009). We are less aware of our environment just before we have an insight. Remember reading about Salvador Dali in Chapter 2? He had some of his best ideas in the brief moment just as he was about to fall asleep. This fine balance of activation and deactivation of brain networks provides the conditions necessary for our brains to juggle the competing demands of various modes of thoughts and allows for creative insights.

Metacognition applied to Creativity

Unique learners

By viewing all learners as having the capacity for Creativity, the Flexible Mindsets model encourages everyone to explore their divergent thinking abilities. To help students explore their strengths and limitations, you may wish to have them respond to questions such as those presented in Table 8.1. These items are part of

Table 8.1 Metacognitive Insights Survey (MIS): Creativity

Creativity	Yes 😊	Sort of 😐	Not Yet ☹️
I work well with others towards common goals			
I like to brainstorm ideas			
I can imagine lots of future possibilities			
I am engaging often and deeply in my areas of interest and my passions			
I like to try out new things			
I readily share my ideas with others			
I want to expand my worldview			
I love when things are messy			
I enjoy taking things apart and building something new			
I want to contribute to the world being a better place			

the Metacognitive Insights Survey (MIS) which we use when we conduct a Flexible Learning Environmental Scan (FLES) (see also Appendix B).

Multiple perspectives

Creativity depends heavily on the ability to shift perspectives (Kozbelt, Beghetto & Runco 2010). This means that, metacognitively, creators need to be aware of and take into account multiple viewpoints. By shifting perspectives, anyone can become open to exploring *What are the possibilities?* and to contributing to original insights. On the other hand, ideas can become too extreme, lack meaning and become inaccessible to others. It is our ability to be aware of the thoughts and mental states of others that allow us to harness, evaluate and modify divergences. As learners interact, a balance is struck between originality and relevance.

Large group discussions often discourage risk-taking due to the stigma attached to being unconventional (Kozbelt, Beghetto & Runco 2010). Rewards, incentives and comparisons further induce anxiety. It is no wonder, then, that many students are reluctant to share novel ideas and insights. The strategies presented in the next section can help to reduce anxiety and make Creativity fun again.

Flexible Mindsets strategies for Creativity

Many teachers are already receptive to novel ideas and use brainstorming and in-the-moment opportunities to respond positively to unexpected responses. Flexible Mindsets strategies are designed to build on these skills to promote the flow of ideas, flexible thinking and originality (Torrance 1972). Here we review three strategies that can be adapted across content areas and development levels:

Strategy #1: *Bending, Breaking or Blending* Making something new out of something old

Strategy #2: *Diffuse Dreams* Diffuse thinking and interleaving

Strategy #3: *Crazy Connections* Metaphorical thinking

Strategy #1: *Bending, Breaking or Blending* (Making something new out of something old)

Creativity does not happen in a vacuum. All new ideas and creations start somewhere. Neuroscientist David Eagleman and composer Anthony Brandt (2017) describe three cognitive strategies that support Creativity: bending, breaking and blending.

Step 1 What are Bending, Breaking and Blending?: Share these simple definitions and examples with your students:

- Sometimes, there is something we do or see every day and then we *change the lens through which it is viewed or add a new twist*. This is called *bending*. Eagleman describes meeting a man with a prosthetic arm. The engineers who designed the prosthetic realised that they could go beyond a normal hand, so they made the hand without tendons, so that it can keep rotating past 360°. Like basing airplane wings on birds, this is an example of taking something from nature and bending it to improve on it. Other examples of bending include modern productions of Shakespeare, Garrett Morgan's three-light traffic light and burrs inspiring George Mestral to invent Velcro.
- At other times, instead of bending, we *fracture something into distinct pieces and then use one or more of them to construct something new*. This is called *breaking*. Examples of breaking include Picasso's art, making shoes out of plastic bottles or using lionfish scales to make earrings.
- If we *start with two or more ideas and merge them*, we are *blending*. Examples of blending include fusion cuisine, mashup songs, jazz, mythical creatures and combining polyester and fibreglass for boat hulls.

Step 2 Research: Have students find, explore and explain examples of bending, blending and breaking in art, engineering, literature and so on. Note that the same inventions used to teach students about the value of mistakes also tell stories of Creativity (aspirin, Post-it Notes, silly putty, Slinky, Velcro and so on).

Step 3 Practice: Assign projects in which students follow the processes of bending, blending and breaking. For younger children, have them take apart toys and create new inventions using a set of those parts or provide a variety of open-ended materials and have students create new art or inventions. For older students, have them dissect a scene from their daily experiences by listing the sights, sounds, smells, tastes, textures. Have them take these ingredients and create a novel setting or story that is their own.

Strategy #2: *Diffuse Dreams*
(Diffuse thinking and interleaving)

Whilst Critical Thinking is heavily dependent on being focused, the psychological states necessary for Creativity occur primarily when the brain is engaged in diffuse mode. Learners often describe the creative process in terms of a journey where the mind wanders freely. They move fluidly from one idea to another, go 'with the flow' and get 'into the zone'. Research by Dr Barbara Oakley and Terrence Sejnowski suggests that we are constantly moving between the focused and diffuse modes of thinking (2018). There is also evidence of an incubation effect that helps us to gain insight by moving from focused to diffuse thinking (Sio & Ormerod 2009).

Step 1 What is diffuse thinking?: Explain to students that *diffuse thinking happens when you relax your attention and let your mind wander, as when taking a walk or daydreaming. It allows us to synthesise knowledge and form new connections between ideas.* Let them know that other students often describe the divergent process as 'making a mess', 'brainstorming', 'throwing out random ideas', 'mixing things up' and 'doodling'.

Step 2 How do we get our brains into diffuse mode?: It is often helpful to share with students about the types of breaks that are helpful. Researchers have divided diffuse mode breaks into three categories (Sio & Ormerod 2009):

- relaxing, such as lounging on soft furniture or listening to music;
- mild activity, such as surfing the internet or doodling; and
- engaging activity, such as reading on an unrelated topic, writing a short essay or digging into other work.

Physical movement and positioning can help by capitalising on the connection between concrete bodily experiences and creative cognition, revealing the aspects of Creativity that are embedded in our consciousness. For example, when considering an idea from two angles, it can be helpful to use the phrase 'on one hand . . . on the other hand . . . ' *in conjunction with* the physical gestures of holding something in each hand and weighing them up. In another condition, researchers sat participants in boxes or next to boxes. People sitting outside the boxes came up with a higher number of creative ideas than those who sat inside the boxes (Leung et al. 2012).

Step 3 Make it happen: Help your students explore the process of drifting into diffuse mode by providing opportunities for mind wandering, structuring breaks and reflecting on their experiences. The following advice may be helpful:

- Prime your brain: before your diffuse mode break, free associate on the topic on which you seek creative insights; capture your initial thoughts by jotting them down, doodling or making video or voice recordings.
- Try out tools such as the Pomodoro® method (Francesco Cirillo 2020): set up a system to alternate between focused (25 minutes) and diffuse modes (5 minutes); play around with the time periods to find the best mix for productivity.
- Build boundaries around the process. To maximise your time spent in focused mode, turn off news feeds, social media accounts and other notifications and potential distractions.

Strategy #3: *Crazy Connections* (Metaphorical thinking)

A metaphor is *something that compares an existing idea with another, unrelated or dissimilar idea*. Metaphors are not the same as analogies because, for an analogy, the two ideas being compared have obvious similarities. With metaphors, the connections are unusual and lead to unexpected insights that result in divergent ideas. Effective metaphorical learning provides distance and incongruity between two ideas to stimulate curiosity and induce personal involvement with ideas. Metaphorical thinking is representative of Flexible Mindsets as it allows learners to view topics from multiple perspectives and understand that ideas can be understood in different ways.

We make sense of concepts and have novel insights by forging connections to something we already know. For example, early automobiles made sense to people because they were described as 'horseless carriages'. William Harvey compared the heart to a pump, which paved the way for his discovery that blood circulates. Here is one way to introduce the use of metaphors.

Step 1 What is a metaphor?: Teach learners a simple definition of the term metaphor. Young children can learn that a metaphor is what we use to find a way that two things are alike, even when they seem quite different. Older students may understand a definition such as something that compares an existing idea with another, unrelated or dissimilar idea. Explain that metaphors help creative thinking in three ways:

- by finding similarities between two topics that, on the surface, appear unrelated;
- by seeing old ideas in new ways; and
- by looking outside of the box and going beyond our comfort zone to seek new ideas.

Step 2 Provide examples: Provide a range of examples of metaphorical thinking, not only in literature, but in science and other areas. Based on grade level and topic, examples might include: time is money; cut the fat; Ridley Scott pitching *Alien* as *Jaws* in space; Dr Martin Luther King's metaphor of black Americans living on "a lonely island of poverty in the midst of a vast ocean of material prosperity"; the food chain; the snow-blanketed meadow; a heart of stone; a snow globe of ideas.

Step 3 Stimulate divergent thinking: When you use a metaphor to link two ideas together, you are combining elements that have little or no logical connection. By breaking the rules of logic, metaphors can open up creative ideas. Furthermore, learners tend to come up with more creative ideas when they wander around randomly, rather than walking in a square or sitting (Leung et al. 2012). Collect, and have your students collect, a wide range of images that remind them of, but are not exactly the same as, a topic your students are studying. Make sure that the images are presented in a range of formats: photographs, clipart, diagrams, cartoons, icons, models, stick drawings and so on. Encourage students to collect images that convey movement and action as they lead to richer metaphors (lawn sprinkler, racing cars, team sports, dancers, birds flying, forest fire, rock climbing, spider spinning a web, leaves falling, waves, clouds, windmills). Set up several stations (desks or wall spaces) and disperse the images among the stations at random. Have the students wander haphazardly around the stations and take pictures or make notes as they ask themselves questions such as:

- What do these pictures remind me of?
- Which visuals could help me understand (and remember) the topic better?
- What connections between ideas are surprising to me?

Step 4 Make a metaphor: Assign your students into small groups. Ask them to select two to three images that they found most engaging. Depending on your learning goals, explain that each group will develop a metaphor that helps them:

- understand and explain a concept in a new way;
- come up with creative solutions; or
- extend a creative idea to engage others in a social, cultural or environmental issue.

Have students discuss the metaphors that best match their thinking and why they chose them. Encourage them to move the images around to find patterns or associations that run through the group's ideas. Depending on your desired outcome and available time, ask each group to capture their metaphorical thinking. They can create a concept map, collage, storyboard, mosaic, model, poem, video or other means of expression. Ensure they emphasise their out-of-the-box thinking and how they 'borrowed' ideas from somewhere else. Ultimately, they will develop the ability to share ideas about questions such as "What's the connection for learning? How can we apply it to worthwhile endeavours? *What are the possibilities?*"

Note that for younger children, we can use a selection of objects and props and have them explore how one thing can serve as a substitution for something else.

Creativity in action: a space junk example from a teenager

At the Intel International Science and Engineering Fair (2015), 15 year old Dana Arabiyat, from Amman, Jordan, decided to create an invention that is both divergent and worthwhile. She explored the issue of space junk which includes parts of old satellites like paint chips and bolts, larger sections of satellites and even whole defunct satellites. One of the reasons space junk should be addressed is that in orbit things move at much faster speeds (28,000 km/h) and, at this speed, even small objects can destroy an entire satellite. As satellite production and use continues to increase, the problem of space trash becomes a future crisis with significant ramifications we can't ignore.

Ultimately, Dana's solution likely sprang from her sense of integrity, ingenuity, persistence and ability to think outside of the box. She created a satellite with a built in radar system that scans for space junk. Thrusters propel the satellite to chase an object and cameras help the satellite to navigate. When within range of an object, a door opens to a super strong trash bin that swallows the junk. When the trash bin is full, it is lowered towards Earth on a cable and the junk is released into the atmosphere where it burns up. The satellite then reels the container back up to continue collecting more trash. Dana's version of the satellite collects bits of debris up to about 50 centimetres across. To broaden the impact of her solution, she thought about how this satellite could be altered for even larger pieces of trash. Dana proposed a version of the satellite with a larger door and a stronger trash bin because the larger pieces of junk would cause more damage to the container when caught.

(Perkins 2015)

Table 8.2 Flexible Learning Activation Checklist (FLAC): <u>C</u>reativity

☐	Students have a shared definition of <u>C</u>reativity as the capacity to ask and answer *What are the possibilities?*
☐	Students can articulate that goal of <u>C</u>reativity is to generate ideas that are (1) imaginative, (2) divergent and (3) worthwhile
☐	Students are aware of their personal strengths and weaknesses in relation to <u>C</u>reativity (refer to Table 8.1)
☐	Flexible Mindsets language is prevalent: unique, imagine, connections, brainstorm, curious, *What are the possibilities?*
☐	Students are exposed to a diverse range of experiences, both experiential and virtual
☐	Work displayed/student portfolios include a wide variety of interpretations, ideas and creations
☐	The physical setting promotes divergent thinking through models of unconventionality and nonconformity, with connections to meaningful goals
☐	Teachers model a shift in priorities to place more value on <u>C</u>reativity by sharing their own learning experiences and how we all can draw on our own <u>C</u>reativity
☐	Grading practices include credit for students' self-reflections about the creative process and out-of-the-box thinking
☐	Possibilities are imagined that make the world safer and more just
☐	Uncertainty is reframed as opportunity

Consider Dana's process and the degree to which she was engaged in Productive Puzzling:

- What do you think may have contributed to Dana's sense of safety for risk-taking? (condition 1).
- Was this puzzle challenging for Dana? Were solutions within reach? (conditions 2 and 3).
- How did this puzzle require Dana to consider multiple strategies? (condition 4).
- What evidence is there that Dana engaged in reflection about her proposed solution and other potential solutions? (condition 5).

By targeting Productive Puzzling directly at <u>C</u>reativity, we can activate the learning that inspires the innovators, expressive artists and social activists of tomorrow. As Maya Angelou teaches us, "You can't use up creativity. The more you use, the more you have" (Elliot 1989, p. x).

Productive Puzzling for <u>C</u>reativity: retrieval practice

As you ponder about this chapter, you may want to use retrieval practice. Cover the right hand column in the first three rows of Table 8.3 and see what you know in regards to the left hand column. Remember, if you struggle then you are puzzling productively!

Table 8.3 Productive Puzzling and Creativity: retrieval practice

QUESTION	WHAT DO YOU REMEMBER?
What is Creativity?	The capacity to ask and answer the question: *What are the possibilities?*
What is the key tool for Creativity?	Novelty
What strategies can we use to build creative capacities? Create specific content-based examples of these strategies that you can use with your students.	1 *Crazy Connections* 2 *Diffuse Dreams* 3 *Bending, Blending and Breaking* 4 ...
What single practice will you shift to encourage students to see themselves as capable and competent as innovators, artists and thought leaders? (the words we use to talk about ourselves and our work, group discussions, grading, etc.)	
How will you get your students to: ■ explore novel and divergent materials and concepts? ■ practice strategies such as diffuse thinking, bending, blending and breaking? ■ create and share inventions, expressive art and innovations?	

References

Adobe. (2016). State of create: 2016 [online]. *Adobe.* [Viewed 15 February 2020]. Available from: www.adobe.com/content/dam/acom/en/max/pdfs/AdobeStateofCreate_2016_Report_Final.pdf

Clapp, E. (2017). *Participatory creativity: Introducing access and equity to the creative classroom.* New York, NY: Routledge.

Eagleman, D., & Brandt, A. (2017). *The runaway species: How human creativity remakes the world.* New York, NY: Catapult.

Elliot, J. (ed.) (1989) *Conversations with Maya Angelou.* Jackson, MS: University Press of Mississippi.

Feldman, D., & Benjamin, A. (2006). Creativity and education: An American retrospective. *Cambridge Journal of Education.* **36**, 319–336. Available from: doi:10.1080/03057640600865819

Francesco Cirillo. (2020). The Pomodoro® technique [online]. *Francesco Cirillo*. [Viewed 4 April 2020]. Available from: https://francescocirillo.com/pages/pomodoro-technique.

IBM. (2010). Global CEO study: Creativity selected as most crucial factor for future success. [online]. *IBM Corporation*. [Viewed 14 February 2020]. Available from: www.ibm.com/downloads/cas/1VZV5X8J

Kaufman, J., & Sternberg, R. (eds.) (2010). *The Cambridge handbook of creativity*. Cambridge, MA: Cambridge University Press.

Kaufman, S., & Gregoire, C. (2015). *Wired to create*. New York, NY: Penguin Random House.

Kounios, J., & Beeman, M. (2009). The Aha! moment: The cognitive neuroscience of insight. *Current Directions in Psychological Science*. **18**(4), 210–216.

Kozbelt, A., Beghetto, R., & Runco, M. (2010). Theories of creativity. In: J. Kaufman & R. Sternberg, eds. *The Cambridge handbook of creativity*. Cambridge, UK: Cambridge University Press. pp. 20–47.

Land, G. (2020). Evidence that children become less creative over time (and how to fix it) [online]. *Idea to Value*. [Viewed 2nd May 2019]. Available from: www.ideatovalue.com/crea/nickskillicorn/2016/08/evidence-children-become-less-creative-time-fix/

Leung, A., Kim, S., Polman, E., Ong, L., Qiu, L., Goncalo, J., & Sanchez-Burks, J. (2012). Embodied metaphors and creative "Acts". *Psychological Science* [online]. **23**(5), 502–509. [Viewed 3 March 2020]. Available from: doi:10.1177/0956797611429801

Oakley, B., & Sejnowski, T. (2018). *Learning how to learn: How to succeed in school without spending all your time studying*. New York, NY: Penguin Random House.

Perkins, S. (2015). Collecting trash in space [online]. *Science News for Students*. 22 May 2015. [Viewed 15 July 2019]. Available from: https://www.sciencenewsforstudents.org/article/collecting-trash-space

Renzulli, J., & Reis, S. (2018). The three-ring conception of giftedness: A developmental approach for promoting creative productivity in young people. In: S. Pfeiffer, E. Shaunessy-Dedrick, & M. Foley-Nicpon, eds. *APA handbook of giftedness and talent*. Washington, DC: American Psychological Association. pp. 185–199.

Richards, R. (2007). Everyday creativity and the arts. *World Futures* [online]. **63**(7), 500–525. [Viewed 3 March 2020]. Available from: doi: 10.1080/02604020701572707

Robinson, K. (2017). *Out of our minds: The power of being creative*. 3rd ed. Chichester, West Sussex, UK: Wiley.

Sawyer, K. (2006). Group creativity: Musical performance and collaboration. *Psychology of music*. **34**(2), 148–165.

Sio, U., & Ormerod, T. (2009). Does incubation enhance problem solving? A meta-analytic review. *Psychological Bulletin.* **135**(1), 94–120.

Torrance, E. (1959). Current research on the nature of creative talent. *Journal of Counseling Psychology.* **6**(4), 309–316.

Torrance, E. (1972). Can we teach children to think creatively? *Journal of Creative Behavior.* **6**(2), 114–143.

SECTION

Flexible Mindsets for equitable education

How can we use the 3C's for the benefit of all learners?

CHAPTER

Equitable classrooms for teaching the 3C's in the context of uncertainty

Someone who used whatever talent she had to do her work to the very best of her ability. And to help repair tears in her society, to make things a little better through the use of whatever ability she has. To do something . . . outside myself.
    (Ruth Bader Ginsburg, on how she would like to be remembered)

If you are like us, you may have chosen your field, in part, because you value the potential power of education to transform lives, promote equity and tackle social injustices with resilience and adaptability. You have probably seen images such as the one in Figure 9.1 that illustrate how antiquated and oppressive systems create the need for us to act in ways that are equitable, rather than equal.

It does not make sense to give every child the same tools and experiences: this only widens the gaps between the haves and have nots. We need to ensure that every child is given an equitable chance to feel competent and capable so they can

Figure 9.1 Equality versus equity

respond flexibly to the unexpected. By equipping them with the tools to learn HOW to learn, we nudge them along the path of becoming self-determining. Only then do we prepare them to adapt to uncertain times, become agents of change, thrive and live their best lives.

It can sometimes be discouraging to look at some of the educational outcomes that plague our communities.

- Sexism is evident in career outcomes: 19% of software developers, 27% of chief executives and 37% of lawyers are female (US Bureau of Labor Statistics 2019).
- In the United States, reading scores are 13% higher for white fourth graders as compared to their black peers (National Assessment of Educational Progress 2019).
- Black students are overrepresented in suspensions and expulsions. Despite being only 16% of the student population, black students represent 32–42% of students suspended or expelled (Office for Civil Rights 2014). In other words, black students are suspended and expelled at a rate that is three times higher than the rate for white students.

Education today is more uncertain than perhaps any other time in history. Educators find themselves faced with more questions than answers. Within this context, opportunities abound. We are poised on a precipice from which we can either fly or fall. This is the ideal time for demystification and transformation of our belief systems. Once we commit to prioritise empathy and equity over the status quo, we can do away with those practices that perpetuate inequities. We must insist upon a better rationale than "That's the way it is" or "Because we've always done it this way." With Flexible Mindsets, educators can take hold of new challenges and craft a better future for themselves and their students.

> In this chapter, we review some of the challenges that teachers have shared with us and that we have also experienced. In each case, we review a scenario that illustrates the inequitable impact of fixed mentalities. Next we provide a simple example of how someone like you has transformed teaching to help prepare their students to cope with uncertainty.
>
> 1. What about the 'high flyers'? The fixed mentalities of high achievers
> 2. 'What if?' versus 'what if?' Relieving anxiety during times of uncertainty
> 3. Students with 'Fix-lexia': learning differences and Creativity
> 4. Persevērance versus Persĕverance: flexibility as an antidote to rigid thinking
> 5. The digital double down and the therapeutic potential of empathy

What about the 'high flyers'? The fixed mentalities of high achievers

In a culture of fixed mentalities, the children with the highest grades often experience major challenges in taking risks for learning. Mistakes and failures are to be avoided at all costs.

> Luc was the top student in his class throughout his education in a small, island community. He instantly recognised what each teacher was looking for and always had the right answer in class. Luc's GPA and SAT scores were impressive enough for him to have his pick of universities. He chose a top-tier, prestigious university in Canada. Upon arrival, Luc was inundated with choices and logistics he felt unprepared for. He selected a heavy course load and took an upper-level course for which he didn't really meet the prerequisite criteria. All of Luc's classes were in large lecture halls filled with hundreds of students. Luc had never struggled with academic content and quickly felt overwhelmed. He had never had to ask for help and felt he would be seen as stupid if he sought assistance. By the time he went home for the December break, Luc was struggling to keep passing grades. He wasn't sleeping properly and often slipped into a 'brain fog' when trying to study. His uncle strongly encouraged Luc to drop at least one course, enrol in the prerequisite class and defer the upper level course to a future academic year. Luc, however, wouldn't take the advice because he thought it would be an admission of failure. He didn't want to take an extra semester to obtain his degree: that would make him a loser, wouldn't it? The hole Luc was digging for himself was getting deeper and deeper.

Students like Luc often start out in kindergarten with curiosity, a desire to explore and a natural affinity for creative pursuits. As they move through a system of traditional fixed mentalities, they are rewarded for correct answers, speed of responses and flawless performances. Their self-identity is wrapped up in appearing smart: regurgitating content, never asking questions that might make them look 'stupid' and preserving the semblance of expending minimal effort. As a result, they engage primarily in safe surface thinking. Just as struggling students develop self-limiting mindsets based on fear of failure, surface thinkers develop self-protective mindsets (see Figure 9.2). They will do the work necessary to protect their 'smart' images, but will not explore beyond their comfort zones. With Flexible Mindsets, self-awareness helps us to set realistic goals and grapple with concepts. Through Productive Puzzling, all learners are inspired to be curious and ask questions, learn from mistakes, attempt multiple strategies and persevere.

Oftentimes, the best strategy for surface thinkers is to set up the puzzle, ask questions, afford time and let the students do the work. In her book *The Having*

Flexible Mindsets for equitable education

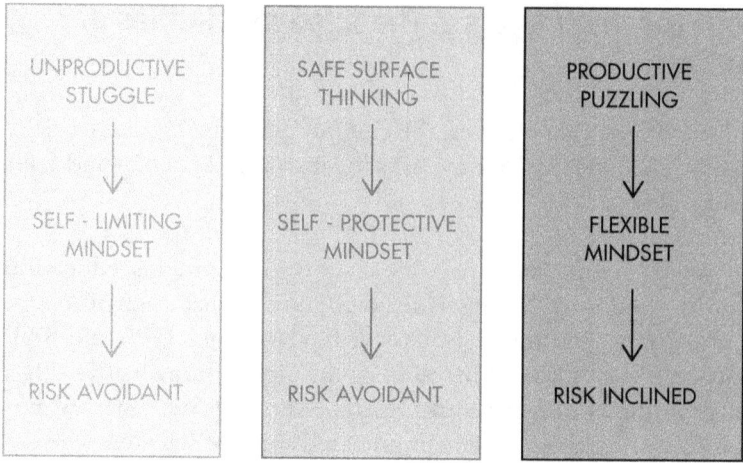

Figure 9.2 Implications of mindsets for diverse learners

of Wonderful Ideas, Eleanor Duckworth emphasised "the virtues of not knowing" (2006). In one of her anecdotes, she captured the experiences of Alec, the ten-year-old student who most educators would be glad to have in the classroom. We present an abbreviated version of her account.

> During the course of the pendulum study . . . the class watched some film in which a pendulum dropped sand as it swung from side to side, thus leaving a record of its travels. One question the students considered was, when a pendulum is swinging back and forth, does it slow down at each end of its swing, or does it maintain the same speed and simply change direction? Alec, who was a bit of a mathematician by inclination, quickly maintained that the pendulum did not slow down at the ends "because there's no reason for it to." The other children tended to agree, because the first opinion came from Alec. . . . [But] [a]fter a while, one child said, "I don't get it. Why isn't it the same all along the straws, then?" . . . Another child said, "There's more at the ends; it piles up at the ends." . . . Gradually the comments added up. . . . At last, one child dared to commit himself: "It has to be slowing down at the ends." And one by one, each child committed himself to an opinion that was the opposite of Alec's. Alec, who was used to being the only one to hold a given opinion, was unconvinced for a long time by their reasons. . . . Finally, Alec was convinced by their reasons and quietly changed his mind. [During a subsequent lesson] Alec put forth another idea during public discussion, again with easy confidence that it would work. It didn't. It was discarded and the class looked for others . . . he said to the teacher . . . "You know I've learned one thing in this class – I don't always have such great ideas." What was new for him was the honest recognition that some of his thoughts might bear a closer look before deserving his commitment to them – they might even benefit from the scrutiny of other children.

> *Flexible Mindsets Guiding Principle #1*: Ask Carefully Crafted Questions and afford time for puzzling, so students can reflect on their learning and become more self-directed.

'What if?' versus 'what if?' Relieving anxiety during times of uncertainty

Too many students spend their days fearing risk, with thoughts of what could go wrong swirling around in their heads. You may remember Jelani from earlier in this book and how his anxiety closed the window for learning. This phenomenon multiplies during times of uncertainty. For example, a University of Oxford survey (Waite, Creswell & Patalay 2020) found that:

- one in five (17%) younger children were afraid to leave the house and worried there would not be enough food to eat during the course of the Covid-19 outbreak; and
- roughly half of younger children (53%) were worried about family and friends catching the disease.

Productive Puzzling is built upon creating trusting relationships and safety for learners to ask questions, make mistakes and take risks for learning. Using Flexible Mindsets language, sharing power and modelling responses to challenges all contribute to trusting relationships and giving learners some sense of control. These measures help reduce the anxiety that is based in uncertainty. Some strategies that educators recommend are listed here.

1. Strengthen connections by: using a shared folder (e.g., Google Classroom) for posting art, other work and positive feedback; holding office hours for students using messaging, a conferencing app or small group virtual meetings; or daily check-ins using emotion emojis or private Google forms (without using checking in as a form of control).
2. Respond to expressed fears by validating feelings, being truthful, encouraging students to seek help and notifying caretakers if you have significant concerns.
3. Focus students on what they can control by reminding them of choices they have; encouraging journaling; scheduling daily exercise; and promoting volunteering time, actions and artwork.
4. Become an Emotion Scientist (Brackett 2019): teach emotional literacy through sharing strategies, encouraging boundaries around media exposure and teaching cognitive distractions that break negative thought patterns (e.g., audiobooks, calming apps, trivia games and mindfulness).

Here is an example of one educator's response to student anxiety.

Will Ehrenfeld (2020) teaches US history at Pathways in Technology Early College High School. He began his teaching career with the desire to make change and inspire his students. After many years of service in the nation's largest school system, Mr Ehrenfeld learned much about the barriers to real reform. Despite this, he has never given up on his goal of inspiring his students. But now his US history course ends in a standardised test that is a graduation requirement. This exam, of course, does not assess inspiration.

As schools around the world switched to remote learning due to the pandemic, Mr Ehrenfeld quickly learned that the traditional structure of school was not working. He thought back to his early teaching, when he spent most of the class time coaching students on their projects rather than providing direct instruction on content. So he sent his students a message which we have abridged:

> After two weeks away from school, I wanted to reach out and try to relieve some of the stress that many of you are feeling. The best advice I can give you is to accept the situation. We are living through a crisis and at times that may consume your attention. You should not stress about my class right now. I hope you can find some enjoyment in learning about history and exploring big questions together, but I also want to be realistic with expectations. So, I am changing my approach. For the rest of the time we are away from school, you will pursue independent research projects. I will walk you through the process step by step over the coming weeks . . . you should not be concerned about your grades right now. As your teacher, let me assure you: a completed project will earn you a 90 at minimum. I want you to explore this work for yourself and your intellectual development, not for a grade. We will review this project on our next video call.
> Thanks, Mr. E.
>
> (Ehrenfeld 2020, para. 19–21)

By giving his students choice over what they want to learn, Mr Ehrenfeld is shifting the balance of power towards a partnership with the learner. This sense of having control over their learning empowers students and helps to reduce feelings of anxiety. This is a simple step that can begin to transform 'what if?' fears about grades into 'what if?' wondering about possibilities.

> *Flexible Mindsets Guiding Principle #2*: Be responsive to the moment through authentic language, power sharing and alleviating stress-inducing demands.

Students with 'Fix-lexia': learning differences and Creativity

Decades of practical experience has shown us that children who learn differently often have strengths in one or more of the 3C's, particularly Creativity. The traditional educational system often communicates low expectations for students with learning differences, thereby further marginalising them. The deficit-based mindsets that permeate traditional educational systems often leave children feeling as if they have to be mended in some way, as if they have 'Fix-lexia'. This can become a self-limiting mindset that precludes a student from asking questions, taking risks and learning from mistakes.

> A few years ago, I was conducting an assessment with Ky'Ano, a curious and engaging ten-year-old who lived with his grandmother. Ky'Ano did well on the initial items, but after the first few items on each subtest, he started interrupting the instructions to ask questions such as "Dr Jules, are grey whales the biggest mammal in the world?" or "Tree frogs stick to the walls, so do they have sticky pads like lizards? Can all frogs climb walls?" At first I thought that Ky'Ano was merely adept at the art of avoidance. But when I asked him what he was experiencing, he explained that he quickly became 'bored' when something was no longer new and had difficulty paying attention because ideas just kept popping into his head. Ky'Ano also completed tests of divergent thinking and performed extremely well. His primary strengths were listed as solving novel problems, making conceptual connections and thinking outside of the box. At the next school meeting, Ky'Ano's teachers were primarily focused on his attentional challenges and reading inefficiencies and wondered whether or not he could cope with the regular curriculum. It wasn't the case that his teachers didn't see or value Ky'Ano's strengths: they simply felt under the constraints imposed by the overreliance on high-stakes testing to assess student performance. I found myself wondering, yet again, about the mismatch between the 3C's that are essential for students to adapt and thrive and whatever it is that we are testing for.

As educators, we can open the door for children with learning differences by leaving the product open ended in both content and means of expression, valuing different ways of thinking and being and showcasing diversity in responses. Following is an example of how one educator has promoted Creativity in a way that can be implemented in either a physical or virtual educational setting. This project-based learning example is described in more detail in the book *Yes, But . . . If They Like It, They'll Learn It!* (Church, Baskwill & Swain 2007):

> As part of an activity on categorising, Olivia Reid's Grade 4 students brainstormed lists of different toys and then grouped them into categories. Responding to comments from her students, Ms. Reid asked her students to create a personal Toy Timeline illustrating their favorite toys at different ages. They developed class graphs, discussed the results and theorised about how different toys might interest a child at different stages. This sparked curiosity that spawned a host of learning activities including:

- Research on the history of toys (children collected photos and examples, wrote about the toys and set up a display).
- Interest in toy ads on television which led to the development of a survey and discussion of results about the frequency of ads and the messages they were sending to the children.
- Investigation of one toy company that revealed concerns about health and safety risks for workers, provoked discussions about different ways that people (citizens) can express their concerns and sparked the decision to write letters of complaint to the company and letters of support for the workers and the production of a video news report about the toy industry.
- Comparisons of the quality and costs of toys, presentations to the class and compiling material for the Toy Report newscast.
- Identification of problems that children had encountered with certain toys, letters to toy companies of students' complaints and suggestions and even some responses back from the toy companies.

In this project, students were engaged in Productive Puzzling. Their curiosity was piqued and extended through personal interests and they used and shared a variety of strategies for research and communications. Students were excited to discover unexpected connections between toys and history, business, child development and other fields. They used the 3C's by thinking critically, tackling complex problems and creating and expressing ideas.

This type of learning does not require any 'special considerations' for students who learn differently. It did, however, require Ms Reid to challenge herself in terms of group organisation, integrating content into the process and having to think on her feet! By meeting this challenge, Ms Reid has made a valuable contribution to Creativity and flexible thinking.

> *Flexible Mindsets Guiding Principle #3*: Leverage strengths and interests to design extended group learning experiences that target the 3C's, so students discover unexpected connections and grapple with ideas.

Persevērance versus Persĕverance: flexibility as an antidote to rigid thinking (pr·suh·veer·uhns versus pr·sev·eh·rents)

We have all seen students who fear failure and lack persevērance. Yet we have also seen students who are inflexible and persĕverate, using the same approach over and over again and tilting at windmills.

In elementary school, Gemma was a straight A student, except for PE. The gym teacher had never seen a more uncoordinated child! The other children found Gemma annoying. She interrupted them, talked on and on and failed to get their jokes. She didn't know how to avoid trouble and was an easy target for teasing and bullying. Even when she had rare friendships, they never lasted. In high school, Gemma struggled with advanced mathematics (anything that depended on spatial awareness) and the more complex questions in language arts stumped her. She could no longer rely on memorising facts and formulas. She kept asking the same questions over and over again, interjected seemingly irrelevant statements into class discussions and resisted different approaches to learning. What had seemed to her teachers to be a child who was bright, but eccentric and unpopular, became a problem student. Eventually, Gemma was diagnosed with a nonverbal learning disorder.

We often associate persĕverance with the cognitive inflexibility of individuals on the autism spectrum: repetitive behaviours, difficulty taking the perspective of others, overcommitment to rules or being hyper-focused on a topic of interest. The reality is that many of our students will have times when they get 'stuck' and need help getting 'unstuck'. They may be unable to move on from a challenging test item, interrupt others, hold on to anger, resist shifts to a different strategy, dispute evidence that contradicts their preconceptions or make the same mistakes over and over again (see Figure 9.3). If we think about it, we all have times when we perseverate.

As we engage in repetitive thoughts and behaviours, we end up in a seemingly unending loop of being stuck. Imagine a tract of mud where we drive a truck back and forth in the same place. Over time, we sink deeper and deeper into the same rut. In the same way, neural pathways in our brain become stronger and stronger, seeking circumstances that recreate the activation of those networks. Persĕveration is the maladaptive version of *neurons that fire together, wire together*.

Figure 9.3 Persĕverance: being stuck in the mud

To counteract persĕveration:

1. Teach metacognition explicitly – "Is 'getting and staying stuck' something I need to work on? When do I get stuck (what is happening around me and what am I feeling?)? What happens as a result of me getting stuck? Does what I'm doing help or get in my way?"
2. Teach perspective taking – "How do others interpret my actions? When I get stuck, does it help or frustrate those around me? What is motivating this person?"
3. Teach self-monitoring – "How will I recognise when I am stuck? What stops me from getting unstuck? What strategies can I use when I am stuck? How can I tell that I am about to get stuck? What can I do to avoid getting stuck in the first place?"
4. Encourage students to use self-talk to walk themselves through problems, verbalise their thoughts about what they want to produce and visualise outcomes.
5. Intervene wisely – if a student is shutting down due to frustration or anxiety, listening and providing space come first, with strategising to follow. Responsive listening includes: validating experiences through neutral observations ("I see your head is down on your desk and I'm wondering if you are stuck"); empathising ("It's frustrating when we feel stuck"); and, lastly, offering strategies.

Next we present an example of a teacher who encourages students to shift into different roles and take into account the perspectives of others.

Sarah Brown Wessling teaches English literature in Iowa and was the 2010 National Teacher of the Year. She shares:

> My ninth graders and I had spent the last forty five minutes doing question for question, point for point, and I had a sinking feeling as I realised this would be our last discussion of Maya Angelou: the posturing of points. Did it really matter if they could recall every 'what' I put in front of them? I thought I had been using themes, such as power, to frame this unit, but actually, I was still teaching the details of a book, not offering for my readers the kind of authentic experience we all crave. I was teaching them how to read for school, not for life.
> (Brown Wessling, Lillge & Vankooten 2011)

To help her students delve deeply into literature, Sarah uses pinwheel discussions where students play the roles of key authors and have teammates backing them up. Her example uses texts by Flannery O'Connor, Gabriel Marcia Marquez and Sherman Alexie and sets up the classroom in a pinwheel configuration (Brown Wessling 2017).

Sarah then uses a set of specific strategies to help students take on the persona of the authors and engage in discourse that reflects multiple perspectives and digs deeply into literary themes.

For examples and details, please watch Sarah's Teaching Channel (Brown Wessling 2017). Note also that this type of exercise can be adapted for younger children by having students play characters from one or more children's stories, with other students acting as panellists.

Pinwheel discussions engage students at a deeper level that is consistent with Productive Puzzling. Trusting relationships are created by allowing students to feel fearless by taking on a persona and having support from teammates. These conversations are a powerful tool for teaching students to ask and answer Carefully Crafted Questions and to find and apply effective strategies for thinking flexibly. This represents a significant step towards all students responding to uncertainty with resilience and adaptability.

> *Flexible Mindsets Guiding Principle #4*: Create opportunities to puzzle through the exploration of different perspectives, so learners can become more flexible thinkers.

The digital double down and the therapeutic potential of empathy

Does technology hold promise for resolving inequities in education? You may have seen articles over the past few years that illustrate the impact of digital divides, particularly under the conditions of remote learning. One such story about a student, 'Grace' from Michigan, appeared in ProPublica (Cohen 2020). We have summarised some of the key details:

> Grace and her mother shared a strong bond and commitment to their community. As she reached adolescence, Grace began to act out and the two had frequent arguments that were about typical teenage stuff. Unaware of other ways to get help, Grace's mother involved the police when Grace became aggressive. As a result, Grace was assigned to and successfully completed a court diversion programme for 'incorrigibility' and agreed to participate in counselling. In November 2019, a neighbour called the police in response to calls for help from Grace's mother, resulting in a charge of assault against Grace. Several weeks later, she was caught on video stealing another student's cell phone. These two charges led to Grace being placed on probation. Thereafter, Grace and her mother participated in individual and family therapy and Grace stayed out of trouble.
>
> Then the Covid-19 pandemic hit and schools moved to remote learning. Michigan's governor suspended the confinement of juveniles who violate probation unless a young person posed a "substantial and immediate safety risk to others." Throughout the US, teachers, families and students struggled with

the upheaval caused by these school closures. Tens of thousands of students failed to log in or complete their schoolwork. Students with special needs were especially vulnerable without the face-to-face guidance from teachers, social workers and others. Grace, who has ADHD, said that, like many students, she felt overwhelmed when online learning began. With limited instruction and structure, she became easily distracted and had difficulty keeping herself on track. During a check-in with her caseworker, Grace shared that she had forgotten to plug in her computer and her alarm didn't go off, so she overslept. A few days later, the caseworker filed a violation of probation against her for not doing her schoolwork. Her teacher clarified that Grace was

> not out of alignment with most of my other students. . . . Let me be clear that this is no one's fault because we did not see this unprecedented global pandemic coming. . . . [Grace] has a strong desire to do well . . . she is trying to get to the other side of a steep learning curve mountain and we have a plan for her to get there.

Despite this, the court ultimately ruled that Grace was in violation of her probation and she was detained at a juvenile facility for not submitting her schoolwork.

Grace is not alone in struggling with remote learning and the challenges that come with fixed mentalities about race, income and disability. A host of complex factors shape technology use in ways that exacerbate existing education inequities. These include:

1. inequitable access to technology, specifically in regards to computer ownership and fast and reliable broadband subscriptions;
2. intergenerational gaps in digital use – families that have been denied access to technology may have limited experiences with software and navigational strategies, resulting in lower rates of digital readiness in children from low income families;
3. purposeful use of devices – lower income, nonprivileged students are more likely to use technology for drill and practice, whereas their more affluent peers use technology for problem-solving and higher order thinking; and
4. underrepresentation in Science Technology Engineering and Mathematics careers, for example, 18% of computer science degrees are attained by women and 12% are earned by Latin Americans.

(Warschauer, Knobel & Stone 2004)

These challenges have been further exacerbated by conditions that have arisen since the beginning of the Covid-19 pandemic. Students, especially those with learning disabilities, are more likely to experience executive function challenges when attempting to plan, organise and complete independent work. The unprecedented rates of unemployment have also meant that many students from middle- to low-income families have had to struggle with the transition to remote learning in tandem with taking on jobs to help their families survive.

There are a number of initiatives that target technological inequities such as large-scale purchasing of laptops or sponsoring internet subscriptions so that all families have access. However, even if all of these physical resources are provided, students like Grace will still be exposed to a system of white privilege with a different, more punitive, set of rules applied to her. Uncertainty holds so much more trepidation for students that look like Grace.

That doesn't mean that we, as educators, are helpless. We do have the power to help all students recognise and resist inequities and cope with uncertainty. Jamilah Pitts (2020) is an educator and equity and justice strategist. She tells us:

> Teaching is great power . . .
>   It is a time to reengage with this powerful profession and work that will lead to necessary change. It is a time to move away from the notion of "returning to normalcy," a normalcy that was rooted in oppression and brokenness. This is a time to reapproach and reimagine teaching as a tool for action and as a vehicle for care. . . . We can and must teach the history and current realities of oppression while celebrating joy, which also is a tool of resistance. . . . It is important to know that teachers can have the hard conversations and teach the hard lessons while caring for students and caring for ourselves, especially if our students are among the marginalized and most impacted. This is human work.

On the surface, it may feel that the solutions to the digital double down should be technological in nature. Technology is a powerful tool; however, if we don't centre our efforts in humanness, it loses its power to make a difference. The answers lie in welcoming students to bring all of themselves to learning, through understanding, caring and empathy. The adults in Grace's life focused on problems, which is the hallmark of fixed and deficit-based mentalities. Imagine how different things could have been if, instead, they connected with her and found solutions that built on what was working in her life.

> Bret Turner, a former first grade teacher, takes the opportunity to lay the foundation for an empathetic classroom by encouraging young children to think more deeply about kindness and how it isn't simply a matter of being kind or unkind. Unkindness is particularly detrimental when hurtful language relates to race, gender, religion or other aspects of a child's identity. These microaggressions reinforce stereotypes and are different from 'typical' six year old unkindness because they are coded messages of disapproval, based on identity. Mr. Turner uses 'the wrinkled heart' as a concrete representation of the damage caused by microaggressions.

The teacher holds up a large paper heart and solicits examples from students of times they were hurt. Each time a hurt is shared, a small part of the heart is crinkled and eventually becomes a crumpled up piece of paper. Next, the opposite is done as students share times they have been lifted up by words and actions, until the heart is unfurled and whole again. But the lines remain etched into the heart, mended, but perhaps never fully healed. During reflection, adults can ask questions such as: "Who is most hurt by a particular statement or action and why? When does an unkindness reinforce a stereotype? How do we show empathy to others?"

(Turner 2019)

> *Flexible Mindsets Guiding Principle #5*: Use the empathy test by asking yourself if your approach creates trusting relationships that promote resilience and adaptability for all students.

As you reflect on this chapter, think about the individual students you teach; Jelani, Luc, Ky'Ano, Gemma or Grace may remind you of one of your students. Where can you begin to shift practices to a more equitable balance and build resilience for responding to uncertain times?

Where can you apply Flexible Mindsets Guiding Principles?

Flexible Mindsets Guiding Principles for equitable classrooms

Flexible Mindsets Guiding Principle #1: Ask Carefully Crafted Questions and afford time for puzzling, so students can reflect on their learning and become more self-directed.

Flexible Mindsets Guiding Principle #2: Be responsive to the moment through authentic language, power sharing and alleviating stress-inducing demands.

Flexible Mindsets Guiding Principle #3: Leverage strengths and interests in designing extended group learning experiences that target the 3<u>C</u>'s, so students can discover unexpected connections and grapple with ideas.

Flexible Mindsets Guiding Principle #4: Create opportunities to puzzle through the exploration of different perspectives, so learners can become more flexible thinkers.

Flexible Mindsets Guiding Principle #5: Use the empathy test by asking yourself if your approach creates trusting relationships that promote resilience and adaptability for all students.

Our educational systems are rife with inequities that are exacerbated by our tumultuous times and uncertain futures. Yet, there are as many opportunities for our students as we and they can imagine. Whether your approach is thoughtful and careful, enthusiastic and spontaneous or somewhere in between; it doesn't matter. If you prefer to dip your toes in the water, just pick one idea from this book; when you are ready, go a little deeper. Or, dive right in, take bold steps and transform your mindset alongside those of your students.

You may sometimes feel you are sailing against the prevailing wind. Remember, you can change tack as much or as little as you choose. There is always more than one course to your destination. If, occasionally, you have to close the door on the outside world and its pressures, give yourself permission to do so. It is within your power, in partnership with your students, to transform learning environments into incubators of possibilities.

References

Brackett, M. (2019). *Permission to feel: Unlocking the power of emotions to help our kids, ourselves, and our society thrive.* New York, NY: Celadon Books.

Brown Wessling, S. (2017). Series Tcher's cut video: Tcher's cut: Pinwheel discussions [online]. *Teaching Channel.* 29th March 2017. [Viewed 14 February 2020]. Available from: https://learn.teachingchannel.com/video/enhance-student-discussions-tchers-cut

Brown Wessling, S., Lillge, D., & Vankooten, C. (2011). *Supporting students in a time of core standards: Grades 9–12.* Urbana, IL: National Council of Teachers of English.

Church, S., Baskwill, J., & Swain, M. (2007). *Yes, but . . . if they like it, they'll learn it!* Markham, ON: Pembroke Publishers.

Cohen, J. (2020). A teenager didn't do her online schoolwork. So a judge sent her to juvenile detention [online]. *ProPublica.* 14 July 2020. [Viewed 15 February 2021]. Available from: www.propublica.org/article/a-teenager-didnt-do-her-online-schoolwork-so-a-judge-sent-her-to-juvenile-detention

Duckworth, E. (2006). *"The having of wonderful ideas" and other essays on teaching and learning.* New York, NY: Teachers College Press.

Ehrenfeld, W. (2020). How this educator is teaching for equity during a pandemic. *Learning.com* [online]. 1 April 2020. [Viewed 26 May 2020]. Available from: https://equip.learning.com/equity-and-justice-during-a-pandemic

National Assessment of Educational Progress. (2019). *NAEP report card: 2019 NAEP reading assessment highlighted results at grades 4 and 8 for the nation, states, and districts* [online]. Washington, DC: National Center for Education Statistics, Institute of Education Sciences. [Viewed 4 October 2020]. Available from: www.nationsreportcard.gov/highlights/reading/2019/

Office for Civil Rights, US Department of Education. (2014). *Civil rights data collection. Data snapshot: School discipline. Issue brief No. 1* [online]. Washington, DC: Office for Civil Rights, US Department of Education. 21 March 2014. [Viewed 23 October 2020]. Available from: https://eric.ed.gov/?id=ED577231

Pitts, J. (2020). Teaching as activism, teaching as care. *Learning for Justice* [online]. 15 May 2020. [Viewed 14 July 2020]. Available from: www.tolerance.org/magazine/teaching-as-activism-teaching-as-care

Turner, B. (2019). Teaching first-graders about microaggressions: The small moments add up. *Teaching Tolerance* [online]. 26 March 2019. [Viewed 14 June 2020]. Available from: www.tolerance.org/magazine/teaching-firstgraders-about-microaggressions-the-small-moments-add-up

US Bureau of Labor Statistics. (2019). Women in the labor force: A databook [online]. *Bureau of Labor Statistics Reports*. [Viewed 4 October 2020]. Available from: www.bls.gov/opub/reports/womens-databook/2019/pdf/home.pdf

Waite, P., Creswell, C., & Patalay, P. (2020). Covid-19: Supporting parents, adolescents and children during epidemics. *University of Oxford* [online]. July 2020. [Viewed 5 October 2020]. Available from: www.researchgate.net/publication/343007260_Covid-19_Supporting_Parents_Adolescents_and_Children_during_Epidemics/stats

Warschauer, M., Knobel, M., & Stone, L. (2004). Technology and equity in schooling: Deconstructing the digital divide. *Educational Policy*. **18**(4), 562–588.

CHAPTER

System disruption for equitable education

In the 1980s, I was fortunate enough to hear Archbishop Tutu deliver a college commencement speech. His inspiration continues to echo the message of true reconciliation. He writes:

> Forgiving and being reconciled to our enemies or our loved ones are not about pretending that things are other than they are. . . . True reconciliation exposes the awfulness, the abuse, the hurt, the truth. . . . It is a risky undertaking but in the end it is worthwhile, because in the end only an honest confrontation with reality can bring real healing. Superficial reconciliation can bring only superficial healing.
>
> (Tutu 2004)

The impact of his words is powerful and spurs me to ask myself, "How honest am I in confronting the truth?" Equitable education in the face of uncertainty is not a finite goal. It requires resilience, flexibility and perseverance. It requires Flexible Mindsets. It involves discomfort and growth on a personal level to change mindsets in a way that is truly transformative. Our children are worthy of it. Our educators are worthy of it. Our future depends on it.

So, if you are ready to extend your impact beyond your classroom, this is where the rubber hits the road. This chapter examines some of the school- and district-level policies and practices that are rooted in systems designed to perpetuate inequities in education and, more broadly, society as a whole. These are the same systems that discourage Flexible Mindsets and reduce the capacities of all students to engage in the 3C's. We move beyond the obvious disparities that result from inequitable funding and resources, to question the assumptions that underlie school experiences and hinder the progress of all students towards perseverance and flexibility.

> Thus far, through Chapter 9, we have offered solutions for promoting Flexible Mindsets within the classroom or school. This chapter examines the broader systemic challenges in education. We:
>
> - begin by discussing the purpose of education as a tool of cultural transmission;
> - critique policies and practices that stifle resilience and adaptability and perpetuate inequities under the guise of a benign educational system, including:
>   - teacher preparation;
>   - the curriculum;
>   - standardised testing;
>   - behaviourism; and
>   - diagnostic and support services;
> - propose steps that can be taken to begin to challenge the status quo, build Flexible Mindsets for uncertain times and disrupt inequitable educational practices and policies; and
> - invite all of us to bring all of ourselves and, together, imagine the possibilities.

Educational purpose and design

According to Kenneth Conklin (2004),

> An education system is the reproductive organ of every culture. Education includes both formal schooling and informal transmission of knowledge, skills and attitudes. Individual members of a society grow old and die, while new members are born and grow to maturity. Yet a society's culture is a living entity which transcends all the society's individual members.

As we reflect back on the premise of this book, we ask again, "What is it that we do to children when we *educate* them?" Education is widely recognised as a powerful tool for cultural transmission. Despite differences in the details, all traditional education systems are seeded in fixed mentalities where there are right and wrong answers and only one way of being. Values and beliefs vary tremendously from one society to another and are largely determined by the dominant culture. Ironically, in the face of uncertainty, when flexibility is most required, schools often cling to the norms that reinforce inequities and deplete the 3C's. Since the system inherently transmits values, the idea that education can somehow be neutral is a myth. Our ideals may tell us that public education functions in the best interests of students and is intended to help students thrive; yet those ideals often come into direct conflict with the doctrine of the status quo.

Economists have long observed the influence of business interests on public systems of education. Industrialists championed universal education efforts such as the Elementary Education Act 1870 in England. Their primary motivation was to take workers from domestic settings and condition them to follow orders, be compliant and remain sober; not to empower them (Mokyr 2001). As such, the goals were not academic or technical skills, but rather social and moral indoctrination. In western society, this influence formed the foundation for the capitalist values that permeate educational systems today, including:

- time as a commodity (punctuality, speed of completing tasks);
- respect for personal space;
- property rights;
- Christian values;
- receptiveness to incentives; and
- individualism and isolationism.

The fallout from this process has served the interests of white, Christian, heterosexual, affluent males by allowing them to:

1. shore up wealth, power and privilege; and
2. perpetuate disparities and injustices in education, health, economics, law enforcement and political systems.

As we described in our preface, not only is content learning artificially parsed out, but we send the message early on that children have to separate themselves into pieces and leave some of those pieces at home. We tell them that, as an entire person, they are not welcome at school. The more there is a mismatch between your culture of origin and the values of the dominant narrative, the more you will be forced to submit to some form of assimilation. This degree of alienation fractures trust and stifles an individual's ability to access the tools for learning HOW to learn and to respond to uncertainty with resilience and flexibility.

Suspect policies and practices

Teacher preparation: the becoming of an educator

so you want every child to learn
first you want to be a teacher
then there are all these things to hold you back (money, hoops, no one leading the way)

> then they try to indoctrinate you into their oppressive belief systems
> whether or not you question these beliefs, they dictate rules for your teaching (power and control, one right way, dominant narratives)
> then you start teaching
> and the machine takes over
> and you sense that this is harmful for everybody
> then you are forced to take workshops that don't address the real problems
> then you feel that you are alone, that you don't have the power to make change
> then you burn out

We can have hopes and dreams for the possibilities our careers hold. As individuals, we can be driven by a sense of purpose and a desire to empower all students to write their own stories. Despite all of this, an inequitable and fixed system, inevitably, leaves us disillusioned.

Given the dissonance between what we want to accomplish and these challenges, how well have we been prepared to accomplish our goals? It often appears that the harsh realities of the education system combine to generate seemingly insurmountable obstacles. How can we as individual educators begin to shift the pendulum in a new direction? We can start with representation and move beyond. In the United States, 82% of public school teachers still identify as white, whereas students of colour will soon make up 54% of all students (US Department of Education 2016). Underrepresentation negatively impacts the engagement and self-worth of many students and also reinforces the values of the dominant system. This is exacerbated when teacher preparation programmes lack coursework and practical experiences that help educators build trusting relationships and provide direct instruction about learning strategies. If teachers don't know how to share with learners about the brain and how it works, how can they help their students be metacognitive, learn HOW to learn and build the 3C's?

These challenges invite us to consider the power of culturally relevant practices that focus on both the academic and personal success of students. These practices lead us to a collective where different ways of knowing and being are the cornerstones of learning communities.

The curriculum problem

In direct competition with the 3C's and Flexible Mindsets, much of the content delivered reinforces disempowerment. A common refrain we hear is the challenges of covering the mile-wide, inch-deep curriculum that many educators face. There is also increasing awareness that issues of nonrepresentation and common myths about learning contribute to inequities based on sexism, racism, ableism and other injustices. This constrains opportunities for all learners to think flexibly, shift perspectives and work together. Here are a few curricular characteristics that contribute to cultural transmission and fixed mentalities and, inevitably, suppress resilience and flexibility.

- **Hegemony:** The curriculum is a tool for disseminating the dominant position of a particular set of ideas and the tendency to view these ideas as 'intuitive' and 'common sense'. This inhibits the articulation and consideration of alternative narratives. Examples include social studies curriculum standards, choices of literature and the history and principles of science and mathematics. *How comfortable are we with exercising hegemonic power over our children and youth?*
- **Eurocentrism:** In addition to hegemony, the act of chopping content into arbitrary fields or disciplines has roots in the so-called Age of 'Reason' or the 'Enlightenment'. Yet today's challenges and tomorrow's uncertainties necessitate holistic approaches to learning. As some universities innovate and construct new interdisciplinary programmes, *how comfortable are we with continuing to compartmentalise and truncate our students' learning?*
- **Paternalism:** Education systems, through a variety of principles and practices, act as a form of governance over students in an outwardly benevolent, but often condescending and controlling way. Paternalism holds the view that students are not capable of learning independently and precludes the flexible thinking that is required for the journey of self-direction. *How comfortable are we with perpetuating controlling policies, patronising children and avoiding power sharing?*
- **Violence:** Hurtful teaching is rarely intentional, but typically arises when we fail to consciously examine our pedagogy. Curriculum violence occurs when authors create a set of lessons that, by nature, are likely to harm subsets of students. For example, there are often instances of curriculum violence during the teaching of economics when comparisons are made between various income brackets. When we gloss over inequities or use judgemental language that reflects capitalist values we risk promoting the viewpoint that poverty is unimportant or that it is somehow the fault of those living in poverty. We erase the historical connections to economic realities that are systemic, as well as the personal narratives of those worst affected. Instances of curriculum violence reoccur throughout a student's educational experiences and can contribute to them becoming retraumatised. *How comfortable are we with curriculum units and lesson plans that reinforce messages of inferiority and may be potentially hurtful?*
- **Volume:** The number of learning objectives in a typical curriculum preclude deeper exploration by valuing quantity of 'boxes ticked' over engagement of students. This overloaded, mile-wide, inch-deep curriculum exerts undue pressure on educators, constricting the time spent on the 3C's. *How comfortable are we with an imbalance between rote, measurable skills and deeper engagement?*
- **Standards-based accountability:** The white dominant culture values quantity over quality, giving rise to the notion that if it can't be measured, it has no value. As such, priorities are directed toward producing easily measurable outcomes. Furthermore, the standards-based curriculum also promotes a sense of urgency

which leaves students feeling like if they don't respond quickly then they aren't smart; and teachers feeling there is neither time to be inclusive, nor the space to encourage democratic and thoughtful decision making. This sense of urgency prevents us from seeing the big picture, prioritising quality of life, being empathetic or considering consequences. It leaves little time to explore the 3C's in any meaningful way. Given these uncertain times, *how comfortable are we defining success by efficiency and easy-to-measure numbers, rather than the 3C's, resilience and flexibility?*

Lest we confuse the curriculum problem as being simply about representation and sensitivity, let's have the courage to question the language echoed within our schools and to seek and hear all voices. This is not a challenge that can be solved by a few workshops on cultural responsiveness and more images of diversity in leadership. Change requires us to apply the process of Productive Puzzling to our own practices and to challenge the system.

Standardised testing

The numbers game of standardised testing is used to classify, categorise and sort students. It treats them as the objects of, instead of the participants in, the school process. For children who don't fit easily into the dominant culture or who learn differently, this form of oppression serves to destroy feelings of self-worth and undermines a sense of competence. Standardised measures discriminate against students based on factors such as learning differences, income inequality and race. They discount student strengths in the 3C's. They are inherently deficit based because they are primarily used to sift, organise and label. Here are some of the ways that testing is counterproductive to Flexible Mindsets:

- *Test development* carries content bias that discriminates on the basis of race, culture and other differences. This is evident in item selection, closed-ended responses and an overemphasis on rote, factual knowledge. Scoring systems penalise students who think outside the box and engage deeply; those who often end up labelled as 'slow processors'.
- *Examiners* are often those who have unconsciously internalised dominant, fixed mentality belief systems. As such, they tend to reinforce those values that disadvantage children from nonprivileged backgrounds. For example, their choice of language and nonverbal cues are likely to be more easily understood by, and therefore more advantageous, to children raised in the dominant culture. Whenever they score a response that is not fully spelled out in the manual, they often reflexively upgrade the scoring for privileged students and downgrade points for students who don't fit the mould.
- *One size fits all* administration, instructions, norm-based scoring and benchmarking are the enemy of individualism and flexible thinking. They are in direct contradiction to the ideals of strengths-based learning and deeper engagement with conceptual understandings.

- *Dehumanisation* often results from the standardised nature of tests where students are given the message that we are separating the 'mice from the men' and that needing help is a sign of weakness. Students are not allowed to use the kinds of strategies that are critical for effective learning. Standard conditions are based on values such as speed, working independently from others and relying on information in memory. These are antithetical to interdisciplinary collaboration, doing research and digging deeply into complex issues.
- *Myths* about the constructs purported to be measured by various tests lead to decisions that are not in the best interests of learners. For example, IQ tests are, at best, incomplete measures of intellectual functioning and yet are often the primary source for making educational decisions without adequate attention to other data. In the case of Flexible Mindsets, they diminish any strengths related to resilience and adaptability.

Ultimately, standardised tests don't centre on students' strengths or measure the capacities that are required for responding to tumultuous times and an unpredictable future: namely, Critical Thinking, Complex Problem-Solving and Creativity.

Diagnostic and support services

Of all the subsystems that operate within educational districts, few are more detrimental than diagnostic and support services. Criteria and tiers are patriarchal ways of thinking and being. By using criteria to categorise children into groups that qualify them for help, we further dehumanise our students. It marginalises strengths such as Critical Thinking, Complex Problem-Solving and Creativity. The processes for identifying, evaluating, diagnosing, producing and implementing education plans for students often serve as more of a bureaucratic exercise than a personalised set of solutions. Some of the challenges students and their teachers face include:

- *Dependent learners* are bred in fixed, paternalistic mindsets by sending messages that students are not capable of success without 'crutches'. In other words, success is not within the students' reach, but depends on help from someone else, which breeds learned helplessness. The more that students receive messages directly or indirectly that they are incapable, the further they experience the disempowerment that depletes initiative and self-directed learning.
- *Deficit-based labelling* occurs whether or not a formal diagnosis is made, especially in environments steeped in fixed mentalities. For some children who have received a formal diagnosis, 'LD' often means they are Learning Disabled, inherently lesser than their 'nondisabled' peers. For other children who have not had an assessment, the children and adults around them inadvertently and subconsciously make them feel as if they are 'LD', meaning Lazy and Dumb. Instead of recognising that all of us have 'LD' (Learning Differences), we have to pathologise children in order to get them services.

- *Barriers* to appropriate services are also prevalent, particularly in schools that are less well funded and mostly serve students from marginalised communities. At the start, a child must actually demonstrate considerable failure before they are identified as needing an alternative form of instruction. We have observed waiting times as long as two years before a psychoeducational assessment is conducted with a student. By the time an Individualised Educational Programme/Plan (IEP) or 504 Plan or Individual Learning Plan (ILP) is formally adopted, there are insufficient human, time and accommodation resources to implement a full plan.
- *'Repairing'* children as if they are engines that are faulty and need to be overhauled. When our interventions aren't working for a child, we offer placements that are increasingly constrictive and punitive in nature or we pathologise entire schools. For example, lessons from 'No Excuses' and militarised schools cut both ways. On the surface, the characteristics of these schools sound reasonable: freedom from bureaucratic interference, measurable goals, leadership from 'master' teachers, contracts with parents, longer school days and years and regular testing. The downside is that success is almost exclusively limited to performance on standardised tests and fulfilling behavioural requirements. As all resources are pooled in this direction, we, once again, lose sight of resilience, adaptability and self-directed learning.

Behaviourism

Where do we begin?

Stars, points, charts, pizza, demerits, detention, suspension, expulsion. These are not tools for teaching children to learn; they are forms of control. When used habitually, these tools are effective as a means for eliciting compliance, obedience, stillness and silence. Yet these aims are the antithesis of what we now know to be the science of learning. Conditioning children to seek external rewards undermines an internal locus of control that helps them believe in their own ability to control themselves and influence the world around them (Rotter 2017). Effective learning involves curiosity, reflection, exploration, multiple perspectives, Carefully Crafted Questions, open-ended outcomes, power sharing, autonomy and flexibility. On the whole, if behaviour modification worked as a tool for learning, we would not be experiencing the current unprecedented rates of school suspensions, high school dropouts, criminal involvement, incarceration and recidivism.

Behaviourism is grounded in values such as authoritarianism, forced choice psychology, white logical empiricism, either/or thinking, conformity, etiquette and correctness. Choices and actions are based on rules, not guiding principles. They are extensions of the practices of early policing where questioning was deterred by exercising power to intimidate, frighten, punish, deny civil liberties and violate.

It is not just simply the case that behavioural tools are unhelpful for learning; it is that they hinder learning. They puncture empathy, keep score, shame, humiliate and dehumanise. They are not empathetic or therapeutic. Using power over someone is often most efficient and effective in taking control in the moment. Yet when we seize power, without getting to the underlying needs of children, we destroy trust. We make them dependent and afraid. In these traditional, fixed mentality cultures, children don't feel safe to ask questions, make mistakes and take risks for learning.

At the end of the day, do we view children as humans to be nurtured or circus animals to be trained?

How do we disrupt?

We have framed Flexible Mindsets as the pathway towards resilience and adaptability in surmounting the uncertainties of today's world and beyond. As individuals, we can make a difference in our classrooms when we welcome the humanness of our students and value all ways of knowing and being. Never underestimate the power of micromoments to change students' lives (Brooks 2020). The smallest of things you do and say can send a message that you care and value a student as they are. These moments are how we begin to shift from where we are now to where we want to be.

Beyond the classroom, our ultimate goal is system disruption that usurps fixed mentalities on a broader scale. As Sonya Renee Taylor says,

> We will not go back to normal. Normal never was. Our pre-corona existence was never normal other than we normalised greed, inequity, exhaustion, depletion, extraction, disconnection, confusion, rage, hoarding, hate and lack. We should not long to return, my friends. We are being given the opportunity to stitch a new garment. One that fits all of humanity and nature.
>
> (Thrive East Bay 2021)

This is messy. It requires struggling with our beliefs, working hard and appreciating the need to do this work alongside fellow activists, collectively. It is not simple, nor is there a single solution. It's not just an add on to existing inequitable systems. It is transformative.

The power to mould minds is both inspiring and daunting. Sometimes we may feel helpless. This is when our choices, words and actions matter most. System disruption requires courage, flexibility and determination. We can find and stoke hope. This section presents a series of steps that, when two or more people get together, can begin to disrupt the system (see Figure 10.1). We encourage changemakers to:

1. reflect on our beliefs and practices (be metacognitive);
2. name what we see, hear and sense (give voice to multiple perspectives);
3. engage in discourse (apply Critical Thinking); and
4. change the playbook (consider multiple solutions for Complex Problem-Solving).

Flexible Mindsets for equitable education

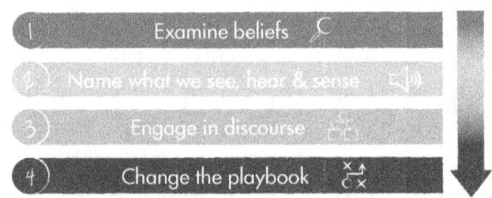

Figure 10.1 Steps for system disruption

Step 1 Reflect on our beliefs and practices (be metacognitive)

Self-reflection is the first step in making change. It is the ongoing and dynamic engine that drives our personal and professional growth towards Flexible Mindsets. There are a number of ways we can explore our contributions to fixed mentalities that are inequitable and deplete our tools for facing challenges.

1. Record your personal *narrative* – sketch, write, sing or video the key events in your life, the identity markers that define who you are as a person and as a professional. *How have these events shaped how you respond to challenges?*
2. Examine your *beliefs* – select two or three different students and note how you respond to them when they are experiencing challenges. Clues about our beliefs can be found in the language we use when we speak with students. *What are some of the beliefs you hold that shape how you respond to different students?*
3. Track your class management *practices* – reflect on how frequently you use techniques such as: preempting disengagement, power sharing, teaching emotion skills, applying traditional behavioural methods, restorative practices. *Which techniques build trust and resilience? Which give students flexible strategies for managing their own learning?*
4. Explore your *role* in your current school and district. When do you listen, take care of others, engage in self-care, speak out, notice, take action? When do you prop up the system and when do you question? *What helps you to be flexible in taking into account others' perspectives and working collectively?*

Step 2 Name what we see, hear and sense (give voice to multiple perspectives)

Once we have raised our own levels of self-awareness, we can use the power of our voices to name what we see, hear and sense. When we give voice to what others think and feel in a safe way, we create the opportunity for them to think 'Huh?' and see themselves or a situation in a different light. By looking and listening for places where there is a hint of openness to questioning, we become an instrument for our collective to reflect on our beliefs and choices as a step towards meaningful change. Empathy and sensitivity give us ways to share what is happening in the moment, observe patterns in each other and our relationships and pull on threads that lead to action. Naming is not to be done in a way that judges or blames anyone. At this level, it is not our job to say whether something is right or wrong or what should be done about it.

Working collaboratively can feel hard because it requires us to recognise what and when to name and then have the courage to do it. We also have to accept that it is going to be messy and that it doesn't work every time. The purpose of naming is to facilitate insights that lead to discourse and powerful change. The gift of naming is that it respects others' perspectives and allows people to make their own discoveries and formulate their own conclusions. Hearing what others see and sense is what helps us stay adaptable and open to change, shift perspectives and strengthen the capacities of Critical Thinking, Complex Problem-Solving and Creativity.

Step 3 Engage in discourse (apply Critical Thinking)

When things don't make sense, we need to begin to question and explore issues more deeply. You may recall from Chapter 6 that Critical Thinking involves asking provocative questions that challenge the status quo. Without it, our minds become suggestible and vulnerable to misinformation. As you engage in discourse, ask yourselves "*Does it make sense?* Are we going to accept this or not? Is this fair or just?" If you're looking for strategies, review those in Chapter 6: use examples and counterexamples to dive deeply into concepts and gain consensus around the criteria you will use to arrive at judgements and make decisions.

This stage of discourse analysis reveals:

- the missing voices in the discussion;
- the myths that need to be debunked; and
- the historical context that has erased the contributions of so many persons.

This allows us to be intentional in:

- seeking out and listening to everyone who has a stake in the outcomes of our committee, collaborative or community;
- counteracting myths and sharing counternarratives; and
- learning powerful lessons from the past that accelerate our path towards resilience and adaptability.

Step 4 Change the playbook (consider multiple solutions for Complex Problem-Solving)

As educators, we have been handed a playbook. Like a player on a sports team, we are told what position to play, what the right moves are and when to run a particular play. As players, we have, until now, been made to run the plays that are called. It is time to rewrite our playbook.

Having engaged in discourse, groups and coalitions are now in the position to identify, describe and solve complex problems. Together, we can review some of the systemic challenges and ask ourselves key questions. We have suggested some ideas next, yet there are no limits to the questions you can generate.

- *Teacher preparation: the becoming of an educator* What are students in teacher preparation programmes being told about the role of an educator (instructor, manager, expert, coach, facilitator, counsellor, parent)? What are they learning about resilience, adaptability and the 3C's? How much research are they exposed to about learning and the brain and how to share it with their students? How are empathy and humanness modelled by lecturers, professors and mentor teachers?
- *The Curriculum Problem* Can all learning objectives realistically be delivered and balanced with deeper engagement? What is the relative emphasis placed on rote skills versus the 3C's? What are the parts of the curriculum that promote the dominant narrative, reinforcing hegemony, Eurocentrism and paternalism? How do accountability measures interfere with learning?
- *Standardised Testing* What is the relative balance between standardised testing and authentic assessment? Which items on your tests are culturally biased? How are standardised test results used to categorise, sort and sift students? How are test results used to highlight students' strengths versus deficit-based levelling?
- *Behaviourism* What are the most frequent class management tools used? What tools are used to encourage, motivate and create trusting relationships for learning? How does your conduct policy address warnings, detentions, suspensions and expulsions? What is the student involvement in constructing classroom norms and school-based policies for engaging them in learning?
- *Diagnostic and Support Services* What are the messages and practices that create dependent learners? How are diagnostic reports and support services used to further harm marginalised students? What is the balance between deficit-based labelling and highlighting the strengths of children who learn differently?

Continue the conversation, select an issue and describe the nature of a specific problem, with all its complexities and contributing factors. Gather potential strategies for addressing the problem from as many perspectives as you can. Keep asking the question *What else can we try?*

Don't forget that strategies can range from prioritising curriculum objectives through policy statements, activism and legislative change. There is no single, correct solution to a complex problem and, depending on the voices around the table, solutions will vary appreciably from one community to another.

As you discuss strategies, imagine alternative solutions. If we take down all our charts and eliminate external rewards, what is it that motivates students in the classroom? How do we create an environment that builds trusting relationships and is engaging?

At this stage, all ideas are welcome and questions of feasibility are deferred. Remember that uncertainty demands that we understand that the world is messy, listen to the perspectives of others and use both ethical principles and cognitive strategies to make the world a better place. These four steps enable teams to change some of the plays that they have been given in their playbook. For example, supplanting learning objectives, replacing standardised tests, changing code of conduct policies or making system-level changes to deficit-based labelling and support services.

Next, if we want to effect change at an even greater level, we can't just change the playbook; we need a new stadium, coaches and players. This is where we need to imagine *What are the possibilities?*

Imagine the possibilities (be Creative)

We started this chapter with the natural tendencies for education to act as a tool of cultural transmission that reinforces the dominant narrative. By highlighting some of the fixed mentality policies and practices that hold learners back from developing resilience and adaptability, we illustrated how traditional education systems are counterproductive for responding equitably to uncertainty. We find hope in these words from Maya Angelou: "History, despite its wrenching pain, cannot be unlived; but if faced with courage, need not be lived again" (1993, lines 74–76).

Any steps you take from this book will start to fulfil the need for Flexible Mindsets to propel students further along the journey of self-directed learning. The previous section is where we explored strategies for changing policies and practices. In this final section, we encourage you to dream big and imagine possibilities beyond changing mindsets within your school or district.

Imagine what your dream school would look, sound and feel like. When we close our eyes, this is what we envision:

> Imagine school is not about control
> Imagine children matter
> And learning is the goal
>
> Imagine there's no shaming
> Empathy rules
> Students resolving their own conflicts
> Learning from mistakes and healing from harm
>
> Imagine sharing power
> Giving choices
> Having students take the lead

Imagine warmth and wonder
Teachers using authentic language
Everyone feeling free to try

Imagine a space filled with belonging
Where children bring all of themselves
And know their voices will be heard

Imagine spaces and objectives
Designed to draw us in
Interests and passions guiding the way

Imagine seeing no limits
Every child's strengths on display
Unique and divergent creations all around

Imagine hearing questions opening minds
Witnessing curiosity as it drives exploration
Children engrossed in puzzling, inspiring dynamic questions
Digging deeper

Feel the energy
Children engaging across ages and stages
Togetherness in learning: the flow of back and forth, give and take

Hear children thinking critically, asking *Does it make sense?*
See multiple strategies and solutions for solving complex problems
What else can we try?
What are the possibilities?
Imagine seeing no limits . . .

As our final thoughts, we encourage you to re-envision teaching as the pathway to empower students to become resilient and flexible as they face the obstacles and opportunities that arise through uncertainty. We hope you have gained a deeper appreciation for the value of the 3C's as critical capacities along the journey of self-directed learning. Experiment with teaching strategies that are based on how the brain learns and that give your students the tools to be adaptive and learn HOW to learn. These approaches can build trust and transform your classroom into a space where everyone can ask questions, make mistakes and take risks for learning. To take Flexible Mindsets to a revolutionary level, change the playbook and disrupt the system, so we can imagine different ways of teaching, learning and being.

We don't have to wait on the world to change: with your help, students can start now to furnish themselves with the messages and tools that activate deeper learning, cultivate perseverance and promote adaptive strategy use. Through Flexible

Mindsets, we can spark self-directed learning as the first step in transforming the system. Help us create a future where thinkers can thrive and we can bring all of ourselves to learning. Now is the time to empower learners to question, solve, imagine.

"Do not get lost in a sea of despair. Be hopeful, be optimistic. Our struggle is not the struggle of a day, a week, a month, or a year, it is the struggle of a lifetime. Never, ever be afraid to make some noise and get in good trouble, necessary trouble."

(John Lewis)

References

Angelou, M. (1993). On the pulse of morning. In: M. Angelou, On the Pulse of Morning.

Brooks, R. (2020). Nurturing resilience in students during challenging times [online]. *35th Annual Learning Differences Conference. 8 October.* [Viewed 8 October 2020]. Available from: https://researchild.org/event/35th-annual-learning-differences-conference/

Conklin, K. (2004). Education transmits a culture (plus a quick look at the separatist agenda of some Native Hawaiian education initiatives) [online]. *Kenneth R. Conklin, Ph.D.* [Viewed 3 March 2020]. Available from: www.angelfire.com/hi2/hawaiiansovereignty/edtransmitsculture.html

Mokyr, J. (2001). The rise and fall of the factory system: Technology, firms, and households since the industrial revolution. *Carnegie-Rochester Conference Series on Public Policy.* **55**, 1–45.

Rotter, J. (2017). *Social learning and clinical psychology.* Eastford, CT: Martino Fine Books.

Thrive East Bay. (2021). Do not go back to normal. [online]. *YouTube.* 18 May 2020. [Viewed 4 November 2020]. Available from: https://youtu.be/Bgc4h-3eDvQ

Tutu, D. (2004). Truth and reconciliation [online]. *Greater Good Science Center.* 1 September. [Viewed 2 October 2020]. Available from: https://greatergood.berkeley.edu/article/item/truth_and_reconciliation

US Department of Education, Office of Planning, Evaluation and Policy Development, Policy and Program Studies Service. (2016). *The state of racial diversity in the educator workforce.* Washington, DC: United States Department of Education.

Glossary

Adverse Childhood Experiences (ACEs) The unrelenting stress caused by poverty, neglect, abuse, household violence, caregiver mental illness, racism, community violence (without supportive adults) that can weaken the architecture of the developing brain (The Center for the Developing Child at Harvard, n.d.).

affinity Something that, when we are in the midst of it, engages us to the point that we don't even notice what is happening around us.

analogy A way to compare two or more ideas that share significant features.

bending When there is something we do or see every day and then we change the lens through which it is viewed or add a new twist.

blending When we start with two or more ideas and merge them.

breaking When we fracture something into distinct pieces and then use one or more of them to construct something new.

challenge Something difficult which requires mental effort and determination. It is the gap between what is already known and what is yet to be learned.

co-creation The receptive and intentional use of student input to inform content delivery, instructional methods and the learning environment.

Complex Problem-Solving The capacity for unravelling an ambiguous puzzle by tackling obstacles and thinking through multiple strategies to find one or more solution(s). It is the ability to ask and answer the question, *What else could we try?*

Creativity The synergy of thoughts to generate ideas that are imaginative, divergent and worthwhile. It is the capacity to ask and answer the question, *What are the possibilities?*

Critical Thinking The capacity that is built through the habit of independent thinking using reasoning, discernment and empathy to analyse issues, decisions, questions and problems. It is the ability to ask and answer the question, *Does it make sense?*

curiosity To be curious is to be inquisitive about the environment, an event, an object, a process or a concept.

diffuse thinking   When you relax your attention and let your mind wander, as when taking a walk or daydreaming. It allows us to synthesise knowledge and form new connections between ideas.

executive function   The interconnected processes we use when we identify a goal, use what we know to figure out what to do, and make it happen.

fixed mentalities   Belief systems that assume that abilities are fixed and that we cannot get smarter.

Flexible Mindset   The dynamic and ongoing interaction between self-awareness, adaptive strategy use and perseverance that empowers learners to evolve and become self-directed.

Flexible Mindsets feedback   Responses that are targeted at specific strategies, are solution-oriented, empathetic and encourage trying a different approach to a problem.

Flexible Mindsets Spiral of Reflective Learning   An ongoing process that educators can use to raise self-awareness and change their mindsets alongside those of their students. This dynamic process ultimately transforms classrooms into environments that are makers of self-directed learners.

goal setting and initiating   Knowing what you want to do and turning your mind's eye towards that purpose.

I CAN messages   The messages that we hear from others and say to ourselves that tell us that our brains can always grow and that we are capable of getting smarter.

interleaving   The strategy of switching between different types of problems. Interleaving is a process where we jumble or mix up a variety of learning activities (the opposite of blocked practice where you study just one topic for a continuous period of time).

metacognition   The awareness of one's own learning and thinking.

Metacognitive Insights   Those 'Uh-oh' moments when we notice that what we're doing isn't working and engage in honest self-reflection about our own learning.

metaphor   A metaphor is something that compares an existing idea with another, unrelated or dissimilar idea.

organising   Making sense of and ordering materials and ideas into a cohesive whole for the purpose of working towards a goal.

partner-centred spaces   Teachers and students share the power and the workload, thereby creating a dynamic characterised by reciprocal flow, lively exchanges and intrinsically driven motion.

planning   Identifying the steps to reach a goal, recording those steps visually and estimating the time each step will take.

Productive Puzzling   Being engrossed in a perplexing problem that is within your grasp but requires thinking, grappling and reasoning.

resilience   A resilient mindset is the product of equipping learners with the necessary tools to work adaptively through change, adversity, trauma, threats, challenges and chronic stress that lie in their pathway towards growth and purposeful self-direction.

retrieval practice   When you quiz yourself and identify what you do and don't know in order to focus your mental energy on the things you haven't learned yet.

self-directed learners Those who actively focus mental energy on their goals and apply their learning to new and meaningful contexts, even when challenged; they are driven by curiosity, a desire to grow and the love of learning.

self-monitoring When you EVALUATE your learning and CALIBRATE your actions.

strategy A deliberate, goal-directed attempt that requires mental effort: what we use when we don't know.

thinking flexibly A learner's dexterity in shifting perspectives and changing course.

working memory The mental workspace where we hold and manipulate information in order to store it in long-term memory, solve problems and produce output.

Appendix A: The Flexible Mindsets Spiral of Reflective Learning

The Flexible Learning Environmental Scan (FLES) is a system for transforming mindsets in schools. The FLES consists of three original tools. It starts with the Flexible Mindsets Spiral of Reflective Learning, the ongoing process that you can use to *raise your self-awareness and change your mindsets* alongside those of your students. This dynamic process ultimately transforms classrooms into environments that are makers of self-directed learners.

A spiral is divided into fifths, each shaded differently to represent one of the five phases: be metacognitive, model, ask questions and afford time, use sharing as a springboard and think on your feet. The spiral illustrates how we can move fluidly between any of the different phases to create classroom environments that are makers of self-directed learners.

After you get started, you can use our Metacognitive Insights Survey (MIS) *to help your students* take the initial steps to reflect on their strengths and weaknesses in reference to the 3C's (see Appendix B).

As your *classroom is transformed*, you can use the Flexible Learning Activation Checklist (FLAC) to track progress (see Appendix C).

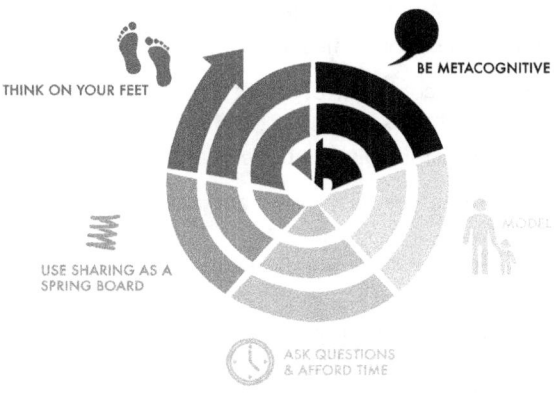

Figure 1.6 The Flexible Mindsets Spiral of Reflective Learning

Appendix B: Metacognitive Insights Survey (MIS)

⚓ reFLEXions®

The focus of this survey is to build your awareness of your own thinking and learning related to Critical Thinking, Complex Problem-Solving and Creativity (the 3C's)

Metacognitive Insights Survey (MIS): Critical Thinking

How much does each statement sound like you?	Yes	Sort of	Not yet
1 I notice contradictions and other things that don't make sense	○	○	○
2 I know my biases and prejudices	○	○	○
3 I am open and flexible about changing my mind	○	○	○
4 I can follow the logic of someone else's argument	○	○	○
5 When making decisions, I weigh up the pros and cons of something	○	○	○
6 I back up my opinions using facts and reasoning	○	○	○
7 My beliefs are consistent with human rights and social justice	○	○	○

Metacognitive Insights Survey (MIS): Complex Problem-Solving

How much does each statement sound like you?	Yes	Sort of	Not yet
1 I view challenges as opportunities to grow	○	○	○
2 I notice when I am confused or don't fully understand something and use that to fuel my curiosity	○	○	○
3 I am able to generate multiple solutions to a problem	○	○	○
4 I am aware of the strategies I'm using and can talk about them with others	○	○	○
5 I respect the perspectives of others when attempting to solve problems	○	○	○
6 When I try to solve problems, my intent is to find solutions that are fair, just and ethical	○	○	○
7 I believe that failure is necessary in order to learn	○	○	○

Metacognitive Insights Survey (MIS): Creativity

How much does each statement sound like you? Yes | Sort of | Not yet

1. I work well with others towards common goals
2. I like to brainstorm ideas
3. I can imagine lots of future possibilities
4. I am engaging often and deeply in my areas of interest and my passions
5. I like to try out new things
6. I readily share my ideas with others
7. I want to expand my worldview
8. I love when things are messy
9. I enjoy taking things apart and building something new
10. I want to contribute to the world being a better place

Appendix C: Flexible Learning Activation Checklist (FLAC)

		The focus of this checklist is to track progress in applying Flexible Mindsets to learning environments
☐	1	Students have a shared definition of <u>C</u>ritical Thinking as the capacity to ask and answer *Does it make sense?*
☐	2	Students can articulate that <u>C</u>ritical Thinking involves independent thinking to analyse (1) issues, (2) decisions and (3) problems
☐	3	Students are aware of their personal strengths and weaknesses in relation to <u>C</u>ritical Thinking
☐	4	Students understand that different questions can be applied to different categories of learning goals and they are able to generate questions accordingly
☐	5	Flexible Mindsets language is prevalent: What would happen if . . . ? I'm not convinced because . . ., pros and cons, I wonder. . . . Is this fair/just? *Does it make sense?*
☐	6	Group and whole class discussions regularly include debates, mock trials, scientific inquiry, moral dilemmas and other criteria-based, decision-making opportunities
☐	7	Grading practices include credit for students demonstrating how they think (not just what they think)
☐	8	Students have a shared definition of <u>C</u>omplex Problem-Solving as the capacity to ask and answer *What else can we try?*
☐	9	Students have a shared understanding of the nature of a <u>c</u>omplex problem (puzzle)
☐	10	Students can articulate that <u>C</u>omplex Problem-Solving involves: (1) puzzles with more than one answer; (2) tackling obstacles; (3) respecting multiple perspectives; and (4) thinking through or trying out multiple strategies
☐	11	Students are aware of their personal strengths and weaknesses in relation to <u>C</u>omplex Problem-Solving

Appendix C

The focus of this checklist is to track progress in applying Flexible Mindsets to learning environments	
☐	12 Work displayed/student portfolios include examples of: strategies attempted that didn't work; more than one strategy to use; and more than one solution to a problem
☐	13 Flexible Mindsets language is prevalent: goal, strategy, other perspectives, persevere, one answer could be . . . because . . ., ethical considerations, *What else can we try?*
☐	14 Small group and whole class discussions regularly include sharing of strategies, discussions of ethical considerations and examples of learning from mistakes
☐	15 Grading practices include credit for students' self-reflections about strategies for problem-solving
☐	16 Particular emphasis and credit is given to solutions that are sourced in empathy, reflect out-of-the-box thinking and put forward counternarratives
☐	17 Students have a shared definition of Creativity as the capacity to ask and answer *What are the possibilities?*
☐	18 Students can articulate that goal of Creativity is to generate ideas that are (1) imaginative, (2) divergent and (3) worthwhile
☐	19 Students are aware of their personal strengths and weaknesses in relation to Creativity
☐	20 Flexible Mindsets language is prevalent: unique, imagine, connections, brainstorm, curious, *What are the possibilities?*
☐	21 Students are exposed to a diverse range of experiences, both experiential and virtual
☐	22 Work displayed/student portfolios include a wide variety of interpretations, ideas and creations
☐	23 The physical setting promotes divergent thinking through models of unconventionality and nonconformity, with connections to meaningful goals
☐	24 Teachers model a shift in priorities to place more value on Creativity by sharing their own learning experiences and how we all can draw on our own Creativity
☐	25 Grading practices include credit for students' self-reflections about the creative process and out-of-the-box thinking
☐	26 Possibilities are imagined that make the world safer and more just
☐	27 Uncertainty is reframed as opportunity

Index

Note: Page numbers in *italics* indicate a figure and page numbers in **bold** indicate a table on the corresponding page.

3C's: in action 84; development of 3; and mental workstation 13
504 Plan 154

active learners 5, 7
Adams, Bryan 69
Adverse Childhood Experiences (ACEs) 44, 45
affinity 29, 133
analogy 109; defined 109; metaphors and 121
analytical problem-solving 103
Apollo-11 mission 28
Art of Inspiring Students to Study Strategically 70
attribution theory 43

Barkley, Russell 16, 18
Beckett, Bernard 9
behaviourism 148, 154–155, 158
benchmark testing 50
bending: breaking and blending 119; flexible mindsets strategies for creativity 119; student's practice of 120
bidirectional questioning taxonomy 74, *74*
blaming trap 11
blending **125**; 3C's in action 84; bending, breaking and 119; student's practice of 120
Bloom's taxonomy 72
Boaler, Jo 60
boredom 29–30
Brackett, Marc 48

brain: blink 117; during imagination 117; and puzzle 26–28; and stress 45
Brandt, Anthony 116, 119
breaking: defined 119; learning and adapting 49; a puzzle 33; rules of logic 122
Brooks, Robert 55

Calvin and Hobbes comic strips 48
carefully crafted questions 34, 68, 72–75, 79–80, 83, 94, 141, 144, 154
Celtic swirl 115
challenge: classroom culture 61; in goal setting and initiating 14; of intergenerational trauma 46; is comprehensible 29; Productive Puzzling balances *33*; and self-awareness 8; social and emotional 48; to spark curiosity 31; in taking risks for learning 133; working memory 15
Clapp, Edward 116
co-creation: exploration and 32; metacognitive awareness 57; partner-centred learning 64; and power sharing 57–59
cognitive science research 70
complex problem-solving 99–101, *100*; activation checklist **111**; and brain condition 103; criteria for **102**; definition of 101–102; metacognitive insights 103–104; in the moment 110; multiple perspectives 105–106; Productive Puzzling for 111; strategies for 106–110

Conklin, Kenneth 148
Covid-19 pandemic: and remote learning 141; and students with learning disabilities 142–143
creativity 114–115, *115*; in action 123–124; activation checklist **124**; brain during imagination 117; definition of 116–117; metacognition applied to 117–118; metacognitive insights survey **118**; multiple perspectives 118; Productive Puzzling for 124–125, **125**; strategies for 119–123; unique learners 117–118
critical thinking 85–87, *86*; in action 95–96; activation checklist **96**; definition of 87; metacognition applied to 88–89; Productive Puzzling and 96, **97**; questions and brain learn 88; strategies for 89–95
curiosity: for deeper thinking and learning 25–26; human spirit and 9; piquing 28–31; and Productive Puzzling 24
curriculum problem 150–152, 158

Darwin, Charles 24
deeper thinking, curiosity for 25–26
deficit-based labelling 153, 159
dehumanisation 153
dependent learners 153, 158
diffuse thinking and interleaving 119, 120–121
Duckworth, Eleanor 59, 134

Eagleman, David 116, 119
educational empowerment 6
educator, becoming of 149–150
effort 11, 27; challenge 32, 70; fixed mentalities 48, 76; feedback and strategies 59, 71, 77, 79; and grappling 94
Ehrenfeld, Will 136
elaboration 88
Elementary Education Act (1870) 149
emotional literacy 135
empathy, therapeutic potential of 141–145
equality *versus* equity *131*
equitable classrooms, for teaching the 3C 131–132; digital double down 141–145; high flyers 133–134; relieving anxiety during times of uncertainty 135–136; rigid thinking 138–141; students with 'fix-lexia' 136–138
equitable education, system disruption for 147; behaviourism 154–155; curriculum problem 150–152; diagnostic and support services 153–154; disrupt 155–159; educational purpose and design 148–149; policies and practices 149–155; possibilities 159–161; standardised testing 152–153; teacher preparation 149–150
equitable learning 8
equity 64, 105, 112, 117, 131–132, 143
error related negativity (ERN) 60
Eurocentrism 151, 158
everyday goals, strategies for **72**
evolutionary value, of not thinking 27
executive function 12–14; definition of 13; and diffuse modes of learning 13; goal setting and initiating 14; key *13*; organising 14; planning and prioritising 14
external markers 59

fear of failure 41, 42–46, 48, 51, 55, 133
feedback, and carefully crafted questions 83; fixed mentalities 43; Flexible Mindsets definition 79; and growth mindsets 59, 77; and mistakes 76; and perseverance 75, 77; and self-reflection 75
fixed mentalities: disregard failures 43; of high achievers 133–134; in most educational institutions 48; for smart students 42
'fix-lexia', students with 136–138
Flexible Learning Activation Checklist (FLAC) 19, **96**, **111**, **124**
Flexible Learning Environmental Scan (FLES) 19, 89, 104, 118
Flexible Mindsets: 3C's in action 84; bidirectional questioning taxonomy *74*; characteristics of 19; of complex problem-solving 101–103; criteria for 83–84; criteria for complex problems **102**; for critical thinking 87, 89–90; defined 19–20; and creativity 116–117; environment 11; and executive function processes 12–14; feedback 75–79; growth mindset 11; guiding principles for equitable classrooms 144; and I CAN messages 9–12; language *62*, 62–65; and metacognition 6–9; model 6, 11, 13, *19*; passive to active learning 5; perseverance plus flexible strategy use 75–79; power of 12; spiral of reflective learning 19–21; strategies for complex problem-solving 106; strategies for creativity 119–123; strategies for critical thinking 89–90; testing is counterproductive 152
Flexible Mindsets Spiral of Reflective Learning: closing the window for learning **51**; get

Index

started with 19–21, *20*, **21**; opening the window for learning **65**; Productive Puzzling 34, **35**; superstructure of Productive Puzzling **79–80**
'Fog Horn' 54, 62

geoengineering 99
goal setting and initiating 14
Grant, Adam 59
grappling 24, 32, 35, 59; to grasp strategy 94–95
Greene, Ross 11, 48
growth mindsets 10–11, 56, 59–60, 75; adoption of 55; construct of 11; feedback based on 77; *versus* Flexible Mindsets 77–79; interpretation of 11; limitations upon an individual's capabilities 11; messages 77

Hallowell, Ned 44, 55–56
Hammond, Zaretta 57
Hannun, Kathy 54, 62
Harvey, William 121
Having of Wonderful Ideas, The 133–134
hegemony 151, 158
highflyers 132, 133–134
Holt, John 48
hourglass image 74, *74*

I CAN Messages 5, 6; Flexible Mindsets and 9–12; in learning environment 50; mindset *9*; value of 12
incongruity 28, 104, 121
Individualised Educational Programme/Plan (IEP) 154
Individual Learning Plan (ILP) 154
intelligence 3, 5, 11, 33, 42–43, 48, 50, 56, 59, 77, 88, 114
interleaving 106; diffuse thinking and 120–121; solve problems flexibly 106–107
invention, impact on lifestyle **93**

Jabbar, Kareem Abdul 25

Kaufman, J. 116
Kounios, John 117

learning 3, 10, 24, 34; academic 27; closing the window for *45*, 46–48; co-creation open the window 57–59, curiosity for 25–26; disabilities 142; equitable 8; from errors/mistakes 11, 60; indicators of 12; knowledge for 7; from mistakes and persevering 12; modes of 13; motivation for active 26; open the window for 24, 32, 54; ownership of 11, 18; partnerships in 20; pathways for 41; and Productive Puzzling 31–32; purposeful 29; self-directed 4–6, 14; and self-monitoring 18; self-reflection about 7, 19–21; strategies for 7, 12; 'sweet spot' for *46*; values that open the window for 59
learning HOW to learn 4, 5, 12, 24, 149

Meltzer, Lynn 78
memory retrieval 103
mental anchor 14, 16
mental processes 7
metacognition 6, *8*; applied to creativity 117–118; and complex problem-solving 103–104; and critical thinking 88–89; defined 9; Flexible Mindsets and 6–9
metacognitive awareness 5
metacognitive insights 7; about ourselves and environmental factors 57; complex problem-solving 103–104; and executive function strategies 89; transforming mindsets requires 78
Metacognitive Insights Survey (MIS) 19, **89**, 104, **104**, **118**
metacognitive knowledge 7
metaphor: of brain 29; thinking 121–123
Miller, Bill 58
mindset: for diverse learners *134*; messages 9; transforming 11
mind's playground 16
mistakes: and failures 60–61; and metacognition 76–77
Motivational Interviewing 58

Oakley, Barbara 120
organising, definition of 14
overt strategy 5

Participatory Creativity 116
partner centred learning 64
paternalism 151, 158
Permission to Feel 48
perseverance: defined 77; *versus* perseverance 138–141, *139*; plus flexible strategy use 78
piquing curiosity: build in time off-task 29–30; comprehensible 29; content and delivery matter 28; inspiration can't be forced 28–29; let it be 30–31
planning: defined 14; and prioritising 14; self-directed learning 20

Index

power sharing, in the classroom 58
problem-solving 3, 7, 48, 69, 100–104; Flexible Mindset strategies for 106; Productive Puzzling for 111
Productive Puzzling 24; balance challenge *33*; challenge and solutions within reach 32–33; for complex problem-solving 111, **111–112**; for creativity 124–125, **125**; and critical thinking 96, **97**; exploring the 3C's 72–75; five conditions for *32*; growth-mindset messages 77; metacognition and mistakes 76–77; multiple strategies 33–34; necessary conditions for 31–32; opportunities for reflection 34–35; perseverance plus flexible strategy use 75–79; superstructure of *68*; teach students about strategies 70–71; trusting relationships 32; valuing practice and struggle 69
productive struggle 24, 80, 133
public humiliation 44

Ramirez, Ainissa 105
Renzulli, J. 116
rescue trap 11
resilience/resilient 10, 11; and adaptability *78*; creativity fosters 116; learners 10; mindset 10
retrieval practice 17, 34; analogical thinking and 109–110; for making meaning 94; Productive Puzzling and critical thinking 96, **97**; Productive Puzzling for complex problem-solving 111, **111**; Productive Puzzling for creativity 124–125, **125**
Robinson, Ken 114
Rollnick, Stephen 58

Sejnowski, Terrence 120
self-advocacy 8
self-awareness 8, 19–20, 133, 156, 163, 165
Self-Determination Theory 5
self-directed learners 5, 9, 19, 21, 24, 69, 87
self-directed learning 4–6, 72; ask questions and afford time 20; be metacognitive 20; model 20; think on your feet 20–21; use sharing as a springboard 20
self-monitoring 14, 17–19, 60, 140
self-reflection 7, 31, 34–35, 63, 72–73, 75, 156
skill, building of 5, 13, 25, 29, 31, 43, 47–48, 51, 56, 61, 63–64, 69, 71–72, 76–77, 119
'slow processors' 43, 152
SMARTS MetaCOG: Metacognitive Awareness Assessment System 77, 78

Socrates, on students' ideas 24
solution oriented language 64
standardised testing 152–153; *see also* equitable education, system disruption for
standards-based accountability 151–152
Stanford University 89
Sternberg, R. 116
strategy: adaptive 19; 'bending, breaking or blending'119–120; complex problem-solving 106–110; 'crazy connections' 121–123; creativity 119; critical thinking 89–90; defined 5, 71; 'diffuse dreams' 120–121; direct instruction 34; flexible 75–76; 'fork in the road' **108**; 'grapple to grasp' 94–95; 'is! is not!' 90–92; how to teach students about 70–71; learner activate and adapt 7; 'mind reminder' 109–110; 'mix master' 106–107; overt 5; perseverance plus flexible *78*; 'prove it' 92–94
stress 45; and brain 45; chronic 46; good 45; and hormones adrenaline and cortisol secretion 46; sweet spot 45, *46*
Sudoku puzzle 32
system disruption, steps for *156*

Taylor, Sonya Renee 155
theory of mind 7
thinking flexibly 14, 16–17, 141
Tutu, D., Archbishop 147

unique learners 61, 117–118

violence 45, 105, 151

Wegner, Gretchen 70
window for learning: asking questions 49; close the *45*, 46–48, **51**; co-creation and power sharing 57–59; hitting the kill switch 54–55; intelligence is not predetermined 59; leaders I see don't look like me 50; long time to answer questions 50; mistakes and failures 60–61; not knowing in our classrooms 61–62; test scores 50–51; trusting relationships *55*, 55–56; values that close 48; values that open 59–62; what we don't know 59; working hard 48–49
working memory 14–16; in action *15*; capacity 15; defined 15; support 15
World History Advanced Placement Exam 50

Yale Center for Emotional Intelligence 48

For Product Safety Concerns and Information please contact our EU representative GPSR@taylorandfrancis.com
Taylor & Francis Verlag GmbH, Kaufingerstraße 24, 80331 München, Germany